Princess Diana

The True Story of the Life & Time of Diana Spencer

(The Amazing Life and Tragic Death of the Queen of Hearts)

Charles Levitt

Published By **Regina Loviusher**

Charles Levitt

All Rights Reserved

Princess Diana: The True Story of the Life & Time of Diana Spencer (The Amazing Life and Tragic Death of the Queen of Hearts)

ISBN 978-1-7780652-4-8

No part of this guidebook shall be reproduced in any form without permission in writing from the publisher except in the case of brief quotations embodied in critical articles or reviews.

Legal & Disclaimer

The information contained in this book is not designed to replace or take the place of any form of medicine or professional medical advice. The information in this book has been provided for educational & entertainment purposes only.

The information contained in this book has been compiled from sources deemed reliable, and it is accurate to the best of the Author's knowledge; however, the Author cannot guarantee its accuracy and validity and cannot be held liable for any errors or omissions. Changes are periodically made to this book. You must consult your doctor or get professional medical advice before using any of the suggested remedies, techniques, or information in this book.

Upon using the information contained in this book, you agree to hold harmless the Author from and against any damages, costs, and expenses, including any legal fees potentially resulting from the application of any of the information provided by this guide. This disclaimer applies to any damages or injury caused by the use and application, whether directly or indirectly, of any advice or information presented, whether for breach of contract, tort, negligence, personal injury, criminal intent, or under any other cause of action.

You agree to accept all risks of using the information presented inside this book. You need to consult a professional medical practitioner in order to ensure you are both able and healthy enough to participate in this program.

Table Of Contents

Chapter 1: Princess Diana 1

Chapter 2: For Onlookers 9

Chapter 3: This Part Of London 15

Chapter 4: When Princess Elizabeth....... 23

Chapter 5: Great Uncle Louis 33

Chapter 6: A Lady Destined To Do Greater Things 48

Chapter 7: The Lady Meets Her Future Prince... 59

Chapter 8: The Princess Becomes A Doting Mother.. 74

Chapter 9: Princess Diana Attends To Her Royal Duties 78

Chapter 10: The Marriage Breaks Down 95

Chapter 11: The Princess' Life After The Separation 126

Chapter 12: The Death Of The Princess Of Hearts 160

Chapter 13: Commemorating Princess Di
.... 183

Chapter 1: Princess Diana

In fairy stories desires do come actual; little girls can broaden as much as marry handsome Princes, and stay fortunately ever after in beautiful palaces, wherein they have got satisfactory youngsters in their very very own, and in time end up Queen, to rule with understanding and grace. But in real lifestyles, in spite of the reality that it seems a fairy tale is being finished out within the complete glare of our cutting-edge-day media age, matters by no means seem to go quite to devise.

THERE ARE few places in the international these days wherein you still discover Princes and Princesses, or for that rely Kings and Queens, but the hundreds of web page traffic who journey to London each year come head to head with Royal Palaces and a facts of succession that dates right yet again to the darkish a while. However, inside the overdue summer season of 1997 people from everywhere within the worldwide gathered in London, in a nation of utter wonder and disbelief, because the most publicized fairy story of the 20th Century came to an abrupt and tragic forestall.

IN THE EARLY hours of Sunday the 31st of August, a beautiful information tale started to unfold, with the arena's press organizations on pink alert. Shortly after middle of the night Diana, Princess of Wales left the Ritz Hotel in Paris and got right into a ready Mercedes on the facet of her companion Dodi Al Fayed. Speeding off into the night time time time to get away waiting newshounds the car crashed at immoderate pace inside the Place de L'Alma street tunnel. The the usage of pressure and Dodi died right away, however the emergency services arrived to discover Diana alive, despite the fact that drastically injured.

AT THE NEARBY Pitie Salpetriere Hospital a hard and fast of Doctors did all they may, but to no avail, and the Princess, who need to, if Fairy Tales are to be believed, have lived thankfully ever after, died at the tragically greater younger age of thirty six, at four am, Paris time.

AS THE PEOPLE of Britain awakened to listen the horrible information in the early morning bulletins, the feel of loss come to be palpable in the course of the kingdom, and indoors hours, floral tributes started out to seem at the gates of Kensington Palace, developing a carpet of colour, the like of which had never been visible earlier than.

THE ONE QUESTION upon each person's lips emerge as pretty truely, how should this have happened? Despite the fact that Diana were divorced from the Prince of Wales for the beyond 365 days and had relinquished her HRH reputation, she come to be despite the fact that formally a member of the Royal own family as the mother of the second one and zero.33 in line to the throne. For the great British public Diana turn out to be as a whole lot England's rose as she had ever been, and along side her improved charity artwork, remained one of the most famous of all the Royals. Almost right away the conspiracy theories started to take flight, and PR for the House of Windsor hit an all time low, at the same time as the adorable young woman, tipped to manual the Royal family into the twenty first Century, have grow to be as an opportunity laid to rest inside the grounds of her ancestral domestic, Althorp in Northamptonshire.

DIANA'S DEATH genuinely marked the remaining of an first rate bankruptcy within the information of the Royal own family, but because the years have surpassed, in desire to fading, her memory has lived directly to inspire each new technology.

YET TO THIS day there are but many questions surrounding the dearth of life of Diana, Princess of Wales, and opportunities aren't any individual will ever recognize for first rate the right chain of activities that introduced about the instant whilst Diana's existence got here to such an premature surrender. Even so, not anything can detract from the impact Diana had on people who knew her for my part, and the relaxation humans, who watched her progress from afar. And as we keep in mind the Princess who supposed the form of terrific deal to such loads of, we'll examine Diana, from her start on the Royal Estate at Sandringham in Norfolk, to seize a glimpse of the real-lifestyles daughter, wife, mother and Princess, upon whom future bestowed the recognition and fortune mere mortals can quality dream of, whilst dealing her the maximum harsh of blows.

WHEN NOEL COWARD located "Very flat, Norfolk", there's no disputing the fact, but to disregard this historic county as a cease result might be to do it a high-quality injustice. With a stunningly stunning shoreline, quaint market cities, richly verdant agricultural land and the navigable rivers and lakes referred to as the Broads, this is rural England at its most endearing, and it's miles the landscape of Princess Diana's starting and adolescence.

SANDRINGHAM, wherein Diana changed into born, is a famous Royal retreat, and as her father, who modified into destined to emerge as Earl Spencer, turn out to be Equerry first to King George VI and then to Diana's destiny mom in law, the Queen, the Spencer own family lived at Park House on the beautiful Sandringham property.

QUEEN VICTORIA PURCHASED SANDRINGHAM HALL, because it have become then seemed, for her eldest son Bertie, the Prince of Wales and future King Edward VII, for his new bride, Princess Alexandra. When the renovations had been whole in 1870 the residence changed into way earlier of its time with gas lighting fixtures, flushing lavatories or even a totally early shower.

TODAY SANDRINGHAM HAS BEEN the private home of 4 generations of sovereigns, with the Queen usually in house over the Christmas holiday until the middle of February. The delightful church of St Mary Magdalene, in which Diana end up christened, is the focal point of a whole lot interest on Christmas morning as it's wherein the Royal circle of relatives worship, bringing out quite a crowd to witness the festive event.

SO, at the same time as The Honorable Diana Frances Spencer end up born at Park House, Sandringham at the 1st of July 1961, the fourth infant of Viscount and Viscountess Althorp, she couldn't have had a higher positioned arrival for a future Princess.

WITH TWO OLDER SISTERS, Sarah, born in 1955 and Jane, born in 1957, whilst Diana seemed on the scene the Althorps could have however been hankering after a son and heir, mainly as in 1960 their 1/3 toddler, a boy, John, died inner hours of his beginning. The gift Earl Spencer, Charles, Diana's younger brother, emerge as born in 1964, to ultimately whole the following generation of this aristocratic own family.

FOR ONLOOKERS, it would seem that Diana have become the maximum fortunate of children, just as she would be perceived as noticeably privileged for the whole period of her tragically short life.

BUT THINGS WERE NEVER as rosy as they appeared. Despite taking component inside the delights of hundred,000 acres of lovable Norfolk geographical region, which once in a while meant going to tea with the Royal friends at the massive residence, existence for the more youthful Spencers come to be about to be thrown into turmoil.

Chapter 2: For Onlookers

THE OLDER SPENCER girls did properly at university, however Diana turn out to be an extended manner extra creative than instructional, and she or he or he struggled to hold up with the excessive necessities set with the aid of way of the use of Sarah and Jane. Diana's self belief turn out to be in addition dented while she broke her arm in a the usage of accident and not like a number of her a long way from educational pals, she wasn't even capable of discover solace in ponies and horses.

AFTER ATTENDING Silfield School in nearby King's Lynn as a day pupil, Diana observed her sisters to boarding university at the age of 9.

A SHY CHILD, Diana have become maximum remembered for her kindness to her fellow university students, mainly those greater younger than herself, as she grew into her teens. But the Spencer ladies confronted quite a wonder when they once more to

Park House for the holidays. In the early Nineteen Seventies their father delivered the present day lady in his lifestyles to fulfill his youngsters, Raine, Countess of Dartmouth, the daughter of romantic novelist Barbara Cartland. If Johnny Spencer had was hoping to create a "satisfied" new own family he have grow to be sadly dissatisfied, as to say that his kids didn't take to Raine as a capability stepmother, might be a huge understatement.

THIS BOMBSHELL for the Spencer youngsters have become then observed through but each one-of-a-kind dramatic change in 1975 whilst the 7th Earl Spencer, Diana's grandfather, died at the age of 80 three. Johnny have emerge as the eighth Earl Spencer, Charles his son changed into now Viscount Althorp and Diana, like her sisters, exchanged her "Honorable" discover for that of a "Lady". The own family moved from Sandringham to the ancestral home at

Althorp, entire with 8,500 acres in Northamptonshire.

FOR THE PAINFULLY SHY DIANA, away at boarding college for maximum of the time, it meant she knew no person inside the vicinity, and subjects had been given worse a one year later whilst her father married Raine in July 1976.

LIKE MANY GREAT ancestral estates in the 1970s, Althorp have become in want of total renovation and the Spencer youngsters believed that Raine have turn out to be dominating the courtroom docket cases, promoting off some of the circle of relatives treasures to fund the refurbishments, which delivered on massive resentment.

THESE WERE critical years for Diana to be suffering such upheaval and her schoolwork really suffered as a stop end result. When she didn't advantage instructional qualifications, and a completing college in Switzerland truly left her home unwell and unhappy, she headed for London, seeking out art work.

THERE WERE masses of properly to do more youthful households in London, searching for suitable "nannies" for his or her youngsters, and as demanding for babies made Diana happy, which in flip meant that she became exquisite at it, she fast carved out a present day existence for herself, notwithstanding the truth that she became hardly extra than a toddler herself. In 1978 on the recommendation of her mom, Diana bought a three bedroomed condominium in Coleherne Court, Fulham, and without delay invited a pick out corporation of women, who've been vintage friends, to residence proportion.

THESE WERE BLISSFULLY glad days for Diana, and notwithstanding the truth that no matter the fact that painfully shy, she commenced to fulfill humans her non-public age and experience the young, rich London scene. After some time she went to artwork on the Young England Kindergarten in Pimlico, which she described as her first "right" challenge, and over again Diana excelled, collectively together together with her more youthful prices adoring her. At last the woman who had craved now not whatever greater in her existence than approval and affection had found fulfillment, searching after other people's kids.

THE LATE 1970S and early Nineteen Eighties were thrilling instances for this new technology of the aristocracy. Benefiting from own family coins to lower lower back them and a London base for Monday to Friday, with a place inside the usa for weekends, the "Henrys" and "Henriettas" of the landed gentry made the Knightsbridge, South Kensington and Chelsea districts of London their private.

HERE, amongst their non-public type, with the gadget of Debutants "out" to do the season now defunct, it have grow to be feasible for those more youthful humans to fulfill appropriate marriage companions, and notwithstanding the reality that instances had been beginning to exchange, the primary reason of an aristocratic girl modified into despite the fact that to marry well, and produce the following era of "Henrys" and "Henriettas".

THIS PART OF LONDON, which integrated Sloane Street and Sloane Square, resulted in this wealthy employer being dubbed "Sloane Rangers", and to this modern a go to to Knightsbridge or South Kensington will bring you into contact with twenty first Century "Sloane Rangers", maintaining up the way of life.

Chapter 3: This Part Of London

WHEN DIANA WAS BORN, her destiny husband modified into simplest a depend of months away from becoming a teenager, and as we've already hooked up, the pair were destined to transport in the equal circles. However, if Diana's privileged childhood is considered to had been rather lonely and remoted, the teens of Prince Charles can handiest be sympathetically seemed inside the equal mild.

ON THE 14TH November 1948 a toddler boy become born at Buckingham Palace to the then Princess Elizabeth, Duchess of Edinburgh and her husband Prince Philip, the Duke of Edinburgh. Christened Charles Philip Arthur George, the Prince modified into their first infant and had the succession run unhindered after the demise of King George V in 1936, the solemn prospect of becoming a King also can in no way have fallen upon the child's shoulders.

BY RIGHTS the number one son of King George V, Edward VIII must have remained on the British throne till his dying in 1972, however his self-discipline to marry the divorcee Wallis Simpson, the woman he loved, prompted his abdication at the tenth December 1936, after no longer pretty 12 months because of the fact the reigning monarch.

AS A CONSEQUENCE, the subsequent in line, George the fifth's second son, the Duke of York stepped into the limelight, to emerge as King George the sixth. With Queen Elizabeth, his accomplice, and extra youthful daughters at his aspect, however his shyness and a nervous stammer, George VI became a miles cherished and respected sovereign. In a hard age, as Britain faced the horrors of World War II, the King shared the experience of his people, as London burned, or even labored with strength of will to triumph over his stammer, which will growth public morale. On the balcony of

Buckingham Palace, he celebrated VE Day with all of London in 1945, and within the placed up-battle era continued to restore the recognition of the monarchy, after the constitutional disaster introduced approximately thru his brother's abdication.

THAT GEORGE VI rose to the disturbing conditions that future had thrust upon him is without query, however it wasn't best his non-public conditions that changed. Elizabeth, his eldest daughter additionally faced the same constitutional responsibilities requested of her father, but due to the fact the Heiress Presumptive she have become given extra time than George VI to prepare for the Royal feature of sovereign. On her 21st birthday she declared that her complete existence might be dedicated to the carrier of her people, and it grow to be a promise that the younger Princess took very significantly truely.

WHEN PRINCESS ELIZABETH married Prince Philip, a member of the Greek Royal circle of relatives and a second cousin, as soon as eliminated, it became precisely as protocol might in all likelihood have dictated, even though it's been advocated that the Princess fell in love collectively collectively along with her good-looking Prince whilst no matter the fact that a female in her teenagers.

AFTER THE ARRIVAL of Charles in 1948, Princess Anne emerge as born in 1950, and regardless of the expectation that Charles would in the future become King, it emerge as but an extended manner off. Nevertheless, on the equal time as his Grandfather's health commenced out to falter in 1951, his mom's accession to the throne changed into turning into more coming near close to than all and sundry decided out. George VI died at Sandringham House on the sixth of February 1952 at the age of fifty six, and some months shy of her twenty sixth birthday the brand new Queen, Elizabeth II became known as upon to do her constitutional obligation, at a time of excellent personal loss, nevertheless grieving for her father.

SO IT WAS that His Royal Highness Prince Charles, elderly honestly 3, became Duke of Cornwall, Duke of Rothesay, Earl of Carrick and Baron Renfrew, Lord of the Isles, Prince and Great Steward of Scotland, and if that wasn't enough for a infant to deal with, he moreover have end up the Heir Apparent.

NOW, must you be thinking what the distinction is amongst an Heir Apparent and an Heir Presumptive, it's honestly quite easy. Prince Charles as Heir Apparent can not be removed from his position as first in line to the throne. Technically on the identical time as George VI have come to be King, if he had long past directly to provide a male heir, his eldest daughter, now Queen Elizabeth II, as Heiress Presumptive, would have needed to offer precedence to a more youthful sibling because of the truth he have become a boy.

WITH HIS MOTHER now excited by way of using topics of usa and his father often away for massive durations of time due to his Naval obligations, honestly as have been the case for Diana, the everyday care of Charles fell to nannies and different individuals of the Royal own family, most significantly his preferred Grandmother, Queen Elizabeth, the Queen Mother. His conditions have been very terrific to Diana's, however the need for parental interest, approval and affection ought to had been simply the equal, no matter how grand the palaces had been that he took place to be living in.

IT'S BEEN SAID on severa activities at some point of facts that with terrific wealth and electricity comes splendid obligation, the historical way of lifestyles of "Noblesse Oblige", and for Charles, issuer, duty and the route to Kingship probable ruled his early life, and for that do not forget, his complete character existence.

CHARLES WAS CREATED Prince of Wales in 1958, consistent with the ancient precedent of the reigning monarch bestowing the pick out upon the Heir Apparent, for the cause that Edward I did, way again in 1301.

IRONICALLY THROUGH THE pages of the records books the perceive of Prince of Wales does now not assure accession to the throne and due to the fact the first investiture of Edward II, seven ought to this thing did no longer pass at once to end up King. Also the immoderate profile feature of the Princess of Wales, the partner of the Prince, has been graced with the aid of some of fascinating women, no longer least Diana, Princess of Wales, the maximum well-known of all of them.

BREAKING with the lifestyle of future monarchs being knowledgeable in isolation by way of the use of manner of tutors,

Prince Charles emerge as sent to school from the age of 8, first off in London, then Kent, and Scotland. Equally as sensitive as Diana have become, Charles is noted to have determined boarding at Gordonstoun School in Scotland hard, miles from home in austere surroundings, wherein his father, the Duke of Edinburgh, had thrived.

Chapter 4: When Princess Elizabeth

CHARLES COMPLETED his education at Gordonstoun, along side phrases at Geelong Grammar School in Australia, leaving with fantastic qualifications including A Levels in History and French. Rather than going directly into the army, as became conventional for the Heir Apparent, Charles went to Trinity College, Cambridge as an undergraduate, reading Anthropology, Archaeology and History. When he graduated with a BA in 1970 he actually made information, because the primary member of the Royal Family to earn a diploma.

NOW CONSIDERED the maximum eligible more youthful guy in Britain, if no longer possibly the complete global, public, and therefore press hobby, became already fueling hypothesis approximately a appropriate healthful for the Prince.

IN 1969 CHARLES'S investiture as Prince of Wales grow to be held at Caernarfon Castle, a few other ancient first, as the ceremony come to be truely held in Wales, and because the occasion became televised, masses of hundreds tuned in to examine the Queen bestow this honor on her eldest son.

IT WAS in the same yr that the Queen took the choice to permit the BBC to movie a documentary about the private lives of herself and the Royal circle of relatives, which includes her two greater youthful sons Prince Andrew and Prince Edward, born in 1960 and 1964. The application proved very well-known with the general public and have emerge as a dignified reaction to the growing media desires confronted via way of the monarchy, however it heralded a brand new and perilous technology that would culminate in the tragic dying of Diana, Princess of Wales, before the stop of the century.

WHEN PRINCE CHARLES embarked upon a Naval profession in 1971, entire with rushing uniform, press hobby in any lady he masses as evolved a friendship with escalated. As a destiny King, he might be anticipated to supply heirs of his personal, and the search emerge as on for a suitable bride for the sailor Prince.

ON PAPER FINDING this form of lady changed into pretty a tall order, in particular at a time when more younger women, whether or no longer excessive born or commoners, had been playing extra independence and sexual freedom than ever in advance than.

IT WAS REQUIRED that a prospective Princess of Wales, and destiny Queen, need to be protestant, now not a divorcee, meet the approval of her future Mother in Law, Elizabeth II, and ideally be a virgin, with aristocratic connections and no colourful past for the press to delve into.

MANY OF THE younger women with whom Charles had been related did no longer meet those exacting requirements, but curiously at the same time as he dated Lady Sarah Spencer, Diana's older sister, within the overdue Seventies a Royal Wedding looked to be at the gambling playing cards. However, despite Lady Sarah's eminent suitability a wedding thought became no longer coming near near and the couple parted corporation, however not in advance than Charles had come into contact with the especially shy, but blossoming Lady Diana Spencer. History, as they are saying, have turn out to be inside the making.

EVER SINCE THE "SWINGIN' sixties", London had emerge as an exciting, vibrant and stylish area to be, and due to the fact the similarly colourful seventies drew to a near, it appeared that Prince Charles have become settling as a substitute with out issues into bachelordom, then a tragedy occurred that pretty actually became his global the incorrect way up.

WHEN THE PROVISIONAL IRA murdered Earl Mountbatten of Burma in a bomb blast, on the equal time as he modified into out crusing in Donegal Bay at the twenty seventh August 1979, they committed a terrorist atrocity that not best bowled over the arena, but additionally robbed Prince Charles of a much cherished Great Uncle, who took place to be, in all possibility, the single maximum large male in his existence. It's been said that the pair stated every precise as "Honorary Grandfather" and "Honorary Grandson", and the younger man constantly listened to what his worldly-sensible relation had to mention.

GREAT UNCLE LOUIS had in reality lived lifestyles to the whole, with a glamorous circle of acquaintance which consist of Royalty and the new generation of celebrities from the Hollywood film employer, counting such luminaries as Charlie Chaplin, Douglas Fairbanks and Mary Pickford amongst his closest friends.

HAVING WATCHED the previous Prince of Wales, Edward VIII, abdicate over a lady, even as being no stranger to the gossip columnists himself through the years, he's reputed to have suggested Prince Charles to enjoy the bachelor existence whilst he may additionally want to, and then marry a younger, natural, green female to ensure the succession.

AS PRINCE CHARLES grieved for Mountbatten he grew to turn out to be to an antique friend, Camilla Parker Bowles for help, going thru also the recognition of his private mortality. Naturally, he preferred to honor the Earl's memory, and it seems he was now prepared to loosen up and discover a Princess of Wales to stand beside him, as he prepared to stand as a bargain because the responsibilities of being Heir Apparent.

WITH THE BENEFIT OF HINDSIGHT, if he need to have married Camilla at that time, then the tragedy of Diana's demise might have been averted, but she grow to be already married, and as we already realize, even though she had divorced her husband, the hazard to the constitutional monarchy, this sort of notably quick time after the abdication of Edward VIII, might have been disastrous.

IN SUCH AN IMPOSSIBLE SITUATION, Camilla, because the Prince's pal, joined the search for a suitable bride. As the 70s gave manner to the 80s, all eyes have become closer to London, and further particularly Coleherne Court, domestic to a set of girls approximately town, truely considered one of whom was of course, Lady Diana Spencer.

AT 19, Diana who had watched the Prince from quite near quarters at Sandringham, emerge as not highly swept off her feet thru the attentions of a complicated, captivating, older man. Diana grow to be invited to enroll in the circle of acquaintance she had constantly been on the point of, such as events on HMS Britannia, the Royal Yacht, inside the route of Cowes week at the Isle of Wight. Today this lovable craft is not in issuer, and can be decided at Leith, the Port of Edinburgh, wherein it is a completely well-known appeal. However, even at a distance such quite a few years later, it's smooth to peer how a smooth-hearted more youthful woman, with little existence enjoy, looking for romance, have to have fallen in love with the Prince who unfold out such an interesting and glamorous new worldwide to her.

BACK IN LONDON a dating among Charles and Diana flourished, with romantic, candle-lit dinners at Buckingham Palace, supposedly in mystery. But it wasn't long in advance than the arena's press installation camp out of doors Coleherne Court and the Young England Kindergarten wherein Diana worked.

LADY DIANA SPENCER changed into demure and charming regardless of the harassment, proving herself in truth discreet, and with this check surpassed, she have become whisked off to look how she could probably cope in Scotland, watching the Prince and his friends fishing and taking photos, as all of the even as Diana persevered to stake her declare to the pick out out, Princess of Wales.

DIANA WAS ALSO INTRODUCED to the county of Gloucestershire, frequently dubbed the Royal County, due to the kind of Royals with u . S . A . Residences there. Charles took Diana to visit Highgrove, the u . S . A . Residence he sold early in 1980, near the pleasant market metropolis of Tetbury. It become in the course of one of the Gloucestershire weekends that Charles took Diana to satisfy Camilla, and together together with his pal's approval, broached the assignment of marriage.

THE OFFICIAL ENGAGEMENT among Prince Charles and Lady Diana Spencer modified into introduced with the useful useful resource of Buckingham Palace at the 24th February 1981. In the pics to mark the occasion, the bride to be wore a blue outfit from Harrods, and it turn out to be glaring for all too see that she loved her fiancée.

IT WAS not practical for the destiny Princess of Wales to flat percentage in Fulham, and at once after the engagement grow to be delivered she moved into Clarence House, the house of the Prince's Grandmother, the Queen Mother.

IN THE MONTHS main up to the Royal Wedding in July, Lady Di fever swept the land. As she requested recommendation from Vogue, in which her sister Jane worked, Diana superior a style which have come to be extraordinarily lady with pie frill collars, pussy cat bows and extended, floral skirts, which the High Street fashion stores were short to emulate. Hairdressers up and down the land were requested to breed Diana's lengthy, blonde, flicked fringe, and the choice for for nannies who have been aristocratic more youthful English women skyrocketed.

Chapter 5: Great Uncle Louis

ALTHOUGH ROYAL WEDDINGS generally desired Westminster Abbey, St Paul's Cathedral became the selected venue, accommodating the tremendous 3,500 traffic. It changed into a fairy story finishing to a present day day love story, and even as the newly weds spark off for Broadlands, Hampshire, the residence of Earl Mountbatten, for the primary night time in their honeymoon, in advance than taking a Mediterranean Cruise aboard the Royal Yacht Britannia, the entire international wanted them well, and expected them to live fortuitously ever after.

AND FOR A WHILE, the Prince and Princess of Wales appeared to have placed the affection and safety they each so desperately desired, with every wonderful. If the general public at big wished in addition confirmation, an statement from Buckingham Palace revealing that the Princess changed into pregnant, 3 months as soon as you have got lower back from honeymoon, ensured that the subsequent era of Royals became more well-known than ever.

WHEN DIANA GAVE delivery to a infant boy, at St Mary's Hospital, London, on the twenty first June 1982, no one can also want to have requested greater of her, and her son, styled, His Royal Highness Prince William of Wales right away took his vicinity as 2nd in line to the throne.

A FURTHER VISIT to St Mary's for the beginning of HRH Prince Henry of Wales, better regarded to the place as Harry, at the fifteenth September 1984 made the future of the constitutional monarchy even extra consistent. It's been counseled that Prince Charles had was hoping for a daughter, however a wholesome son, zero.33 in line to the throne, have turn out to be another time, all every person should have reasonably requested of the Princess of Wales.

THAT DIANA, Princess of Wales loved her sons is beyond question, but as she fulfilled her Royal responsibilities, whether or not or no longer based at her London domestic, Kensington Palace or Highgrove in Gloucestershire, the strain modified into starting to show. By the mid-eighties there was already hypothesis that every one come to be not nicely, in the returned of those high-quality gates, among the Prince and his Fairy Tale Princess, no longer helped by means of the use of the glamorous experience of style Diana had superior, as she grew into one of the international's maximum cute women.

WHEREVER THE PRINCE and Princess of Wales went, at domestic or distant places, the crowds who flocked to look them had been continuously more inquisitive about what the Princess became sporting, in preference to what the more severe minded Prince had to say. However, Diana paid a high price for her popularity as a fashion icon, stricken by an eating disease that turned into most in all likelihood Bulimia Nervosa.

IN JUST A FEW short years the lovely English rose who had promised to breath new lifestyles into the Royal Family, were stifled via responsibility and protocol, and Charles, who had generally tried to comply with the motto of every Prince of Wales, "Ich Dien", that means "I Serve", located himself right once more in which he had started out out, earlier than Diana had agreed to marry him.

WHAT HAPPENED NEXT IS WELL DOCUMENTED thru newspaper and tv facts, as Charles another time grew to end up to Camilla Parker Bowles for consolation, and Diana looked for solace in what she idea to be a discreet affair.

AS HEAD of the Royal own family, the Queen faced a constitutional catastrophe every bit as explosive as the abdication of Edward VIII, which led to her father turning into King lower back in the 1930s. Matters deteriorated similarly and through using 1992, after the harm down of her daughter Princess Anne's marriage and the separation of her 2d son Prince Andrew from his associate, Sarah, Duchess of York, the Queen described this as an Annus Horribilis, which translates from the Latin as quite absolutely a terrible 12 months. Added to hundreds family turmoil, Windsor Castle, the location the Queen regards as her proper home, changed into broken via way of the use of fireside and earlier than the one year have become out the Prince and Princess of Wales had additionally separated.

AS THE WORLD'S press appeared on Diana endured to live at Kensington Palace, gambling time there at the aspect of her "boys". Charles spent pretty a few time at Highgrove in Gloucestershire, in which the younger Princes had lots of opportunity to make the most of the stunning nation-state, whilst they were with their father. Just as is the case for all households that face a marital split, these were tough instances, and for the Prince and Princess of Wales, struggling to find preference for the sake of the youngsters, the everyday press interest did now not a few element to make things any less complicated.

HOWEVER, irrespective of her afflicted non-public instances Diana continued to art work tirelessly for charity, campaigning to enhance public belief of AIDS patients and spotlight the horrible destruction due to landmines, as she fought for a international ban on those cruelly devastating weapons of war.

IRONICALLY, this honestly well worth, immoderate profile stance of the Princess introduced approximately the Royal circle of relatives some trouble, specifically whilst Diana hit the headlines as she tried to carve out a today's life for herself. It changed into now extraordinarily now not going that

Diana need to although turn out to be Queen, however it wasn't conclusively resolved, and the general public adoration that she generated persisted undiminished, and Prince Charles as america's destiny King grow to be all the time going to discover himself overshadowed thru Diana. Eventually the couple's divorce end up finalized in 1996, a year and three days earlier than Diana's lack of lifestyles at the streets of Paris.

AND SO, we go back to wherein we started out out this remembrance of Diana, with the entire international in surprise at the dearth of this virtually great more younger girl.

ON A FINE SEPTEMBER MORNING, London basking in early autumn daylight, prepared to bid Diana a completely final farewell. Her funeral was held at Westminster Abbey at eleven.00am on Saturday the 6th of September 1997. The Royal own family were all in attendance alongside the

Spencers, led with the aid of Diana's greater younger brother Charles, now the Earl. As have become only proper and right, the principle interest have become to useful aid Diana's sons, William and Harry, so regardless of conspiracy theories abounding and an element of antagonism leveled at each the press and the Royal circle of relatives, the funeral of Diana, Princess of Wales became as dignified as it turn out to be moving.

AFTER THE SERVICE, watched via hundreds of masses round the arena, Diana's mortal remains were carried on an amazing journey home, to Althorp in Northamptonshire. All the way from London's familiar landmarks, northwards, the funeral cortege grow to be greeted by means of way of truly lots of normal dad and mom, ready to pay their last respects to the People's Princess.

EVEN ALONG THE verges of the M1 motorway entire households joined collectively to mention their fond farewells, and by the time Diana eventually reached the gates of Althorp for the closing time, the cortege emerge as greater than an hour overdue.

UNDERSTANDABLY DIANA'S FAMILY favored to bury her wherein she want to now not be trouble to press intrusion, and her grave couldn't be greater personal, on an island within the middle of the Oval Lake inside the grounds of Althorp. In the years considering, those closest to Diana had been capable of visit her grave in absolute privacy, which as her sons face the full glare of publicity that ruled Diana's person life, no question they've got very a brilliant deal desired this.

NEVERTHELESS, it's been tough for the masses and hundreds of those who may additionally want to have moreover desired to commemorate the anniversaries of Diana's lifestyles and dying, with nowhere specific to accumulate. The gates at Kensington Palace wherein such plenty of floral tributes appeared manner once more in 1997 will regularly be wherein people choose to place plants. But a memorial in one of the extraordinary church homes like Westminster Abbey, wherein her funeral happened, or St Paul's Cathedral, in which she married, might absolutely show popular with internet web page site visitors who desire to remember Diana with thoughtful contemplation, and as her memory lives on, who can say what the destiny could likely bring.

HOWEVER, for masses human beings a excursion spherical america to quietly stroll within the footsteps of this unforgettable Princess, will usually be a totally unique and profitable experience.

FROM THE MAGNIFICENT Sandringham Estate in Norfolk to the lovable Althorp House in Northamptonshire, the ones first-rate Stately Homes masses part of the state's ancient beyond, have instances while they will be open to the general public. Also, a go to to Gloucestershire will show very interesting. Despite Highgrove, the home of Prince Charles now not being open to the general public, the first-rate, neighboring market metropolis of Tetbury is fascinating, particularly whilst you rely up the kind of "By Royal Appointment" symptoms over the stores. And of route those parents with an hobby in Diana, revel in following the progress of her sons, Prince William and Prince Harry, so what will be nicer than savoring a pint of quality English Ale wherein the Princes have been diagnosed to partake of the hospitality after they're staying at Highgrove?

EVERYWHERE DIANA WENT, she touched the lives of those she came into contact with, bringing pride and choice to wherein it turn out to be most wanted, but if you really need to enjoy the real spirit of this elusive butterfly, then London is the area to transport.

BEGINNING WITH BUCKINGHAM PALACE, you may stroll down the Mall following the direction Diana took to St Paul's Cathedral on that eventful July morning, leaving the palace as Lady Diana Spencer, to move again because the Princess of Wales, and destiny Queen.

AS A POINT OF INTEREST, the Spencer own family name is established to the dazzling Spencer House, which offers guided excursions on the Sundays it's open to the overall public.

WHEN THE FIRST Earl Spencer have turn out to be a prominent society determine once more in the 18th Century, this neo-classical treasure located him on the coronary heart of London, clearly simply in the course of Green Park from Buckingham Palace. Although loads of years later Lady Diana Spencer lived in a contemporary flat very distinctive to the grand facade of the metropolis residence; Spencer House is regardless of the truth that a well timed reminder of Diana's impeccable ancestry, in her very very personal right.

BY CONTRAST A TRIP to Coleherne Court will normally enhance a grin, remembering the vibrancy of Diana as a blossoming bride-to-be, courted through her Fairy Tale Prince. And certainly a go to to Harrods is an absolute want to. Here you can find the stylish designers that Diana loved as a woman about town, however an awful lot, loads more. There is a permanent memorial to Diana, Princess of Wales and Dodi Al Fayed, mounted vicinity with the useful resource of the historical shop's proprietor, Mohamed Al Fayed, the daddy of Diana's accomplice who died in conjunction with her on that fateful night time in Paris.

THE OFFICIAL PRINCESS of Wales Memorial Fountain in Hyde Park emerge as opened via the Queen in 2004, to represent Diana's tremendous affinity and openness with people from all walks of lifestyles. However, the Fountain has now not been without its critics, and plenty of experience a memorial close to Diana's Kensington Palace home, an extended manner greater appropriate. Kensington Gardens have continuously been related to Peter Pan, as it's in which the author JM Barrie met the little boys who stimulated him to jot down down his masterpiece.

HERE THE DIANA, Princess of Wales Memorial Playground recreates the vicinity of Peter Pan and is a becoming tribute to a Princess who had the sort of unique manner with children.

AS OUR JOURNAL draws to a near, this is probably the right location to do not forget Diana, Princess of Wales. For an all too quick length of information she lit up the sector, and shone so colourful that her legacy, as you've observe for your self, lives on. And likely the most treasured present bequeathed via Diana to the kingdom are her sons, Prince William and Prince Harry. Diana's willpower to help them lead happy, fulfilled lives, understanding that their parents loved them, is an prolonged-lasting testomony to an English rose at the way to blossom for all time. Yet the tale of Diana, Princess of Wales simplest goes to show that there's no predicting what the future would likely hold for any folks, and despite the fact that we will continuously revel in unhappiness for a existence out of region so tragically younger, Diana will all of the time be remembered, wherein it subjects maximum, in the hearts of those for whom she ought to were proud to be Queen.

Chapter 6: A Lady Destined To Do Greater Things

Young ladies frequently dream of growing up as princesses wearing tiaras and incredible gowns and living in a fort and assembly a handsome prince whom they may marry once they turn 18. At a time and age even as princesses and princes and queens and kings are greater equated with children's fairy tale storybooks, Diana Spencer effects have end up the Princess of Wales and Queen of People's Heart.

- Throughout her life, British newspapers and guides spherical the sector have to function Diana and the whole thing approximately her on a every day foundation. With a smile that so captured the general public, she attended to her princess obligations and motherly roles, seemingly happy in her married lifestyles. She became typically visible together together with her husband, Prince Charles, regularly shaking hands with the human beings she met and speaking with them with such popularity as even though she and that character have been the best ones around.

- Therefore, it became a marvel at the same time because the country observed, from Diana herself, of the way unhappy her marriage grow to be and the way the royal circle of relatives became choking her. Diana resented the strict protocol to which she need to post and the way she end up treated thru the human beings of the family, in particular Charles whom she hoped would love her and look after her. This described her regular search for a man to provide her love.

- But this did no longer save you her from doing what she cherished: sporting out out and assisting the people whom the society rejected. Coming from a broken family, Diana have to experience the ache of these people, and he or she or he felt that it changed into her obligation to acquire out with a hug and a actual interest to their plight. This brought her towards the loads in a manner now not seen in advance than, without a doubt now not maximum of the royal own family. She stepped down her pedestal, and even even as stripped of her turn out to be aware about, Diana did not prevent supporting people.

- But the records of her lack of life took the kingdom through using way of hurricane. How ought to a woman so younger, and great starting to revel in happiness inside the arms of someone who in fact cherished her, be stripped of her existence? It seemed unfair. And it was satisfactory after her lack of existence that it end up found how masses the Britons, and the people spherical the sector, fashionable and loved Diana. It turn out to be a sworn statement in itself of the way Diana, in her brief life, touched the lives of many.

Childhood and Growing Up Years

Unhappy Childhood

The person whom we have were given referred to as Diana, Princess of Wales, modified into born Diana Frances Spencer on July 1, 1961 in Sandringham, Norfolk in an aristocratic family. She turn out to be the fourth toddler of the Viscount and Viscountess Althorp (nee Frances Ruth Roche). Her father, Edward John Spencer, modified into the 8th Earl Spencer. The Spencer circle of relatives is most of the Great Britain's oldest and most essential households and is cautiously allied with the royal own family for generations.

Diana while she have become a little one

- The circle of relatives was hoping for a male son to be born to preserve on the Spencer name as the couple's 1/3 son, John Spencer, died interior 10 hours of his starting. They were looking forward to a son, and so it took a week earlier than they belief of a name for his or her new child daughter. Diana turn out to be named after a Spencer ancestress and her mom and grew up in Park House near the Sandringham belongings. Park House grow to be owned through the use of manner of Queen Elizabeth II.

- The choice to have an heir brought strain to the Spencers' marriage as the older individuals of the own family favored to realise why Lady Althorp stored generating girls. It modified into said that Lady Althorp modified into despatched to Harley Street clinics in London to attempt to determine the purpose of the "problem." It changed into a totally humiliating enjoy, specifically to Diana's mom who emerge as proud and hard-minded, and Charles Spencer, Diana's youngest sibling, said that it become probably the foundation of the divorce because of the fact they did not get over it.

- Diana changed into first-class 7 even as her parents separated. Her mom had an affair with Peter Shand Kydd and left the circle of relatives. She remembered that her father loaded suitcases in the vehicle and Frances drove a long manner from Park House. Diana lived with Frances in London on some sports activities throughout her parents' separation, however her father had refused to let Frances return to London with Diana at a few stage inside the Christmas holidays.

- In 1969, the Spencers divorced. Lord Althorp received custody of the youngsters, the courtroom docket docket figuring out toward Frances' affair. Frances' mom, Lady Fermoy, testified closer to her, and this helped the court to decide to permit custody of the youngsters to Lord Spencer.

Lord Spencer and Frances should marry their respective companions, but the divorce left an emotional scar at the younger Diana.

- All these things have been though fresh in her mind. She could not forget about how her mom cried all of the time, how her father's lonely silences have become too massive and the way she and her siblings had been left inside the care of severa nannies. Diana remembered all too well that after they were given domestic from school, there'd be a modern nanny searching earlier to them. She additionally hated being shuttled among her parents, and the separation modified into too much for her more youthful brother, Charles, who ought to cry himself to sleep.

- Added to those became Diana's guilt that she wasn't born a boy, some thing that her dad and mom waited all along to preserve on the Spencer name. It grow to be moreover embedded in her thoughts that she turned into best a nuisance to have spherical. Diana longed for hugs and kisses, but she become given a list from a toyshop. She by no means desired fabric topics. And no matter the truth that she became born and grown right right into a rich circle of relatives, she had a totally unhappy childhood.

- Later on, in a mystery taped interview, Diana could keep in mind going through an unhappy youth. She said that her parents were "busy sorting themselves out" and that one time, whilst she turned into hiding in the again of the door, she discovered her father slapping her mom during the face. She additionally stated that in her adolescent years, she didn't have a boyfriend because of the fact she needed to hold herself very "tidy" for what modified into coming her manner.

School Years

Diana first attended the Riddlesworth Hall in Norfolk, an all-ladies college. It became noted that she did no longer shine academically, and so she changed into moved to a boarding college at The New School at West Heath in Kent. Here she grow to be appeared as a terrible student, mainly because of the truth she failed all of her O-stages two times. But she did excellently as an finished pianist. The college moreover identified her wonderful network spirit. Shortly after, her father commenced a courting with Raine, Countess of Dartmouth. In 1975, Lord Spencer have become the Earl Spencer, and Diana obtained the identify Lady.

Young Diana

- In 1976, Lord Spencer and Lady Dartmouth married in London. As Countess Spencer, Raine end up unpopular together with her stepchildren, mainly Diana and her more younger brother, Charles. She even went as a long manner as to name her stepmother

Acid Raine. But there have been media reviews suggesting that Diana had already reconciled with Raine at the time of her loss of life.

- Diana changed right into a shy woman, but she turned into interested in track and dancing. In truth, she preferred to come to be a dancer however, as future may have it, she have end up a princess as a substitute. She became moreover interested by kids, and this have emerge as the inspiration for what she might also turn out to be unexpectedly earlier than marrying the Prince of Wales.

- In 1977, she in short attended faculty on the Institut Alpin Videmanette in Switzerland. This have turn out to be the time whilst she met her future husband, who modified into then in a dating with Diana's older sister, Sarah. Diana excelled in swimming and ballet, and had favored to enroll in the Royal Ballet as a professional ballerina. She studied ballet for a while, however then she grew too tall for the career.

Jobs

In 1978, Diana moved to London and lived in her mom's flat for some time as Frances end up in Scotland the whole time. Shortly after, her father purchased an rental at Coleherne Court in Earls Court for £50,000 as an 18th birthday gift for her. She and her flatmates lived there until 1981. She ultimately enrolled in a cooking beauty, at her mother's encouragement, however she did now not turn out to be an adroit prepare dinner.

Diana as a nanny and nursery university instructor

Chapter 7: The Lady Meets Her Future Prince

The Royal Engagement

When she changed into sixteen, Diana met Prince Charles for the number one time on November 1977 while her older sister, Sarah, added collectively with her the Prince in Althorp. In his late 20s, Prince Charles come to be a first rate seize. He have become a glamorous determine, constantly visible on high-quality uniforms, doing volatile subjects. But Diana changed into no longer impressed. In fact, she said,

"First impact modified into, God, what a unhappy guy. And he got here in along together with his Labrador. My sister have become throughout him adore it become a horrific rash, and I concept, God, he ought to in reality hate that. I saved out the manner. I don't forget being a fat, podgy, non-makeup, unsmart lady, however I made quite some noise and he favored that..."

Diana knew Prince Charles for a long time as he had a courting along with her older sister. At approximately this time, Prince Charles, in his early 30s, have become underneath an growing stress to marry. Diana become already 18 through this time, and he or she or he or he met the Prince for the second time at a friend's residence. Her accurate family historical past, vibrancy and cheerfulness caught the Prince's hobby, and he took an interest in her in some unspecified time in the future of the summer season of 1980 once they have been both visitors at a rustic residence party and she or he or he watched him play polo.

Prince Charles and Lady Sarah Spencer, July 1977

- Their courting advanced and Prince Charles invited Diana for a crusing weekend to Cowes on the royal yacht Britannia. He furthermore invited her to Balmoral, the Royal Family's Scottish residence, to fulfill his circle of relatives. Elizabeth II, the Duke of Edinburgh, and Queen Elizabeth The Queen Mother acquired her.

- The had a whirlwind romance. After about seven months of relationship, Prince Charles proposed on February 6, 1981 within the blue sitting room of his pied-a-terre at Buckingham Palace. Other humans claimed that Charles in reality proposed to Diana in Bolehyde Manor's – Camilla and Andrew Parker Bowles' mansion – garden.

Diana turned into to transport on a 3-week journey to Australia and Prince Charles favored to use the adventure for Diana to make up her mind. But Diana typical and decided on the most vital ring from a tray of jewelry. Their concept modified into saved mystery for the subsequent weeks; it have end up official on February 24, 1981.

When the press positioned out that Prince Charles had a brand new woman buddy, the paparazzi commenced following Diana everywhere she went. They might probably secret agent on her via her rental home windows. She had a tough time coping with individuals who typically had binoculars educated on her. And although it can have been tempting to get away to the privateness of her mom's Scottish home, Diana determined on to preserve a ordinary lifestyles. She faced cameras and reporters whenever she stepped out of her flat or out of her paintings. She left her approach as a kindergarten training aide and moved to Clarence House the night time earlier than the expert announcement of the couple's engagement.

Princess Diana and Prince Charles on their engagement day

On February 24, 1981, they brought their engagement from Buckingham Palace. Prince Charles and Diana had been a photo of a truly best couple. In an interview wherein they professed their love for every different, Prince Charles said,

"…truly extraordinarily glad and glad…I'm amazed that she's courageous sufficient to take me on."

When requested whether or not or now not or not they had been in love, Diana responded with a quick "Of route" on the identical time as Prince Charles introduced, "something in love manner." Diana had in reality come from her enjoy to Australia, and there has been no communication among them on the same time as she modified into away. Diana said that she pined for him, however he in no way rang her up. While they had been all smiles, simplest Diana's recollection, published years after her loss of life, might probable shed slight to the fact that something changed into wrong at this degree.

A Fairy Tale Wedding Fit For A Princess

The Wedding Ceremony

Millions of humans spherical the arena have been excited as they awaited the televised marriage ceremony of Lady Diana to Charles, Prince of Wales. Some had been ready to appearance what she became going to place on on her wedding ceremony day, at the same time as others have been thrilled that they'd be able to trap a glimpse of the princess-to-be. Some have truly come from an extended way places handiest to be part of the marriage of the century.

- On the morning of July 29, 1981, the procession commenced out from Clarence House, with 4,000 police and multiple,2 hundred navy officials handling the group. It changed into expected that million spectators protected the route of the procession from Clarence House to the St. Paul's Cathedral in which the wedding might take area.

- Like a cutting-edge-day Cinderella, however with trumpets blaring, Diana, now 20, arrived at St. Paul's Cathedral in a glass teach along with her father. They were escorted with the aid of the usage of five hooked up navy police officers. Diana emerged from the coach and become welcomed by using way of way of cheers from the institution, and the spectators noticed how lovable she changed into, and her get dressed with a very lengthy educate have come to be the state of affairs of discussions from that day on.

- With the Trumpet Voluntary, she began out the 3-and-a-half minute walk up the red-carpeted aisle along with her father, Lord Spencer, with the beneficial aid of her aspect. There were 3,500 people in St. Paul's Cathedral that morning, which incorporates Queen Elizabeth II, Prince Philip, and the Queen Mother. The wedding turn out to be held at St. Paul's in preference to at Westminster Abbey because of the fact the preceding provided more seating and allowed an extended procession thru the streets of London.

- Diana seemed radiant as she took her father's arm and walked down the aisle, smiling to the faces she exceeded with the beneficial aid of. It changed into a traditional Church of England marriage ceremony issuer that have become presided via the use of Most Reverend Robert Runcie, the Archbishop of Canterbury, and the Very Reverend Alan Webster, the Dean of St. Paul's Cathedral. It became billed as a "fairytale wedding" that about 750 million humans worldwide watched, and this determine rose to billion while the radio target marketplace is introduced in.

Princess Diana and Prince Charles stroll down the aisle of St. Paul's Cathedral

- Perhaps because of sheer tension, Diana's nerves had been given the higher of her and she or he reversed the order of Prince Charles' first names. Instead of saying Charles Philip Arthur George, she stated Philip Charles. Even Prince Charles muddled his non-public vows, pronouncing "thy items" in choice to "my worldly objects." They left out "obey" from the bride's bridal ceremony vows. While this way of lifestyles changed into turning into more and more common inside the wellknown public, it become via hook or by means of criminal debatable in a royal marriage ceremony.

After the ceremony, each Prince Charles and his bride, now Princess Diana, emerged from the cathedral and rode the open-crowned usa landau which would take them to Buckingham Palace for a dinner for 100 and twenty. The crowd cheered due to the fact the couple waved and smiled. Diana changed right right into a image of the luckiest bride within the global while Prince

Charles seemed good-looking and glad on their bridal ceremony day.

A short even as beyond one, the famous couple and their households seemed at the balcony to greet the collected site visitors, a way of life that began out inside the course of the time of Queen Victoria and persevered through way of the couple's elder son, William's wedding ceremony to Kate Middleton. Princess Diana recalled how overwhelm she changed into to appearance the lots and hundreds of people who amassed to look at them that day.

The royal couple kisses on the balcony of the Buckingham Palace

And following manner of life and shouts from the human beings under, Princess Diana and Prince Charles kissed. It grow to be the handiest second that the people had all been searching beforehand to. There became a superb roar from the gang. They then retired in the palace for toasts and a wedding dinner for a hundred twenty family visitors.

On that very same day, the couple departed for the number one degree of their honeymoon. They rode the landau with a "surely married" sign and were driven over Westminster Bridge to get the teach from Waterloo Station to Romsey in Hampshire.

The Dress

Any wedding will now not be whole with out the choice of dress. As predicted from royals, you wager that a woman to get married, an awful lot extra a princess-to-be, goes to region on now not actually an high priced marriage ceremony get dressed however a number of as a way to make her look cute. What Diana would wear on her marriage ceremony day become stored secret, and it would only be decided out on the day as a conventional surprise for Prince Charles and the world.

As Diana emerged from the train, flash bulbs right right right here and there began out flashing. It have become the maximum photographed event of the day, but 2nd best to the occasion on the identical time as she and her groom may emerge from the cathedral after the ceremonies. All eyes were at the dress that she selected, and it simply did now not disappoint.

Princess Diana's dress indeed made her appear like a princess. It became stated to price £9000 and was designed thru the use of Elizabeth and David Emanuel. The marriage ceremony dress become a gasp ball meringue dress with large puffed sleeves, a frilly neckline, and a entire skirt manufactured from ivory and silk taffeta. It became also made with vintage lace, hand embroidery, and contained greater than 10,000 pearls and sequins. The get dressed turned into famous for its 25-foot educate. As quickly as Diana stepped out of the train, it modified into apparent that her get dressed have become complete of creases. It turn out to be criticized with the aid of a few, but irrespective of the reality that, Diana carried herself elegantly and gracefully. Diana additionally wore a tiara over her veil. The tiara emerge as a Spencer family heirloom, and the veil became nearly 8 meters long.

Her Prince Charles, already ready in the cathedral, wore the overall dress uniform of a naval commander. He appeared good-looking and speeding, however these days, it changed into Diana who captured the eyes of the area. It turn out to be her huge day.

The Ring

Diana's wedding ring end up much less complex than her engagement ring, but it have grow to be made from the soft nugget of Welsh gold that have grow to be mined at the Clogau St David's gold mine. Apparently, this changed into the equal nugget that supplied rings for the Queen, the Queen Mother, Princess Margaret and Princess Anne. The ring emerge as engraved on the inner with: "I Love You, Diana."

The Cake

No marriage ceremony is entire without the wedding cake. The royal couple had 27 cakes. The legitimate wedding ceremony cake have grow to be furnished with the useful resource of the Naval Armed Forces. David Avery, the top baker at the Royal Naval cooking school in Kent baked the cake and it took 14 weeks. The bottom layer on my own took 12 hours to bake.

The marriage ceremony cake

Avery had overseen the making of two equal desserts. One changed into a reserve clearly in case the alternative became broken in transit. The Classic Celebration Cakes in Cheshire, which supplied bridal ceremony desserts for the very last 5 reliable royal weddings, additionally provided desserts for the wedding.

- The wedding cake modified into five layers and greater than five feet excessive and embellished with the Prince and his family's royal coat of fingers. You can also see at the cake the couple's first initials and a sprig of roses, lilies of the valley and orchids.

The Honeymoon

On the equal day of the marriage, Prince Charles and Princess Diana took the teach to Romsey in Hampshire and stayed at Broadlands, the circle of relatives home of Prince Philip's family, the Mountbattens. The 2nd a part of the honeymoon changed into spent at the royal yacht Britannia, which the couple boarded on the Rock of Gibraltar in which a few 30,000 people noticed them off.

Chapter 8: The Princess Becomes A Doting Mother

The Best Mother in the World

The Palace brought Princess Diana's first pregnancy on November five, 1981. She overtly mentioned her pregnancy with members of the click corps. In January 1982, Diana had an twist of fate. She fell down a staircase at the same time as she changed into 12 weeks into her being pregnant. Sir George Pinker, the royal gynecologist, modified into brief summoned. Diana suffered severe bruising, but her little one became brilliant.

- Princess Diana gave beginning to a healthful little one boy on June 21, 1982, at St. Mary's Hospital in Paddington, London.

The boy grow to be named William Arthur Philip Louis. Despite criticisms, Diana decided to take William, a toddler then, on her first crucial tours of Australia and New Zealand. Diana admitted that she did no longer intend to take William, until Malcolm Fraser, the Australian immoderate minister, encouraged it. It changed into additionally inside the path of those trips that her recognition among humans have grow to be apparent.

The royal couple, with Princess Diana wearing the little one Prince William

- The couple had their 2nd son years after William, on September 15, 1984. They named him Henry Charles Albert David, but turned into popularly referred to as "Harry." Her pregnancy with Harry have end up a time while she and Prince Charles had been the closest.

- Princess Diana changed right into a dedicated mom. She gave the number one names of her sons, disregarded a royal family nanny and decided on one which she chose. She became also cautiously worried with the lives of her kids, selecting their colleges and their garb and taking them to highschool as regularly as her time table universal. She determined directly to join up them to school with distinctive kids in preference to privately taught.

- Diana had said of her sons,

- "I love my sons. I could be lost without them."

She might likely often be photographed collectively with her sons. Motherhood modified into without a doubt for Diana, and it modified into a completely exciting feature. They could probable regularly spend afternoons looking Prince Charles play polo. When they had been in Highgrove, their weekend home, Diana would probably frequently play cowl-and-are searching out with them. She also taught the guys to be confident and expressive, and that paid off due to the fact at a younger age, William and Harry were now not shy even as speakme with adults. Harry have end up recognized for his kindness, at the same time as William favored to be ordinary.

- There's absolute confidence, in her sons' eyes, that Diana come to be the tremendous mom inside the international. Prince Harry might later talk approximately how Diana have grow to be their "father or mother, pal and protector" who may additionally want to in no way allow her unfaltering love flow into unspoken or undemonstrated. Even after her divorce with Prince Charles, Diana's being a mother to her sons did no longer forestall there. She changed into continuously visible collectively along with her favored kids. Although the divorce changed into miserable, it changed into Princes William and Harry who made her glad.

Chapter 9: Princess Diana Attends To Her Royal Duties

Finding Her Role as a Princess

As a princess, Diana modified into predicted to take care of her duties alongside her husband. She changed right into a younger mother then, thrown into the spotlight for marrying the British heir to the throne. She had the maximum difficult time the number one week after their honeymoon at the equal time as she needed to learn how to be a royal in a single week. She had no formal education in any way, but no individual helped her with what have end up predicted of her.

- Diana had a tough time managing the instantaneous recognition that came together with her marriage. She was once an difficult to understand individual, but then she have grow to be the Princess of Wales, mom to her youngsters, media toy and member of the royal circle of relatives all on the identical time. She said it turn out to be difficult enough to control for one character.

"I didn't need to do anything by myself. I modified into too apprehensive. I suggest, the concept of me doing whatever by myself…despatched tremors, so I caught with some thing Charles did…but the pace became top notch…It didn't get less difficult. I truly had been given used to what people had required from the Princess of Wales."

But Diana appeared to have decided a way to behave like a royal all on her very very own. On the BBC Panorama interview with Martin Bashir in 1995, he said about the information opinions that Diana changed into left to address her new recognition on her very very own. Diana said it have become how she professional, such as that the media had been everywhere and she or he or he should have to discover ways to swim or sink speedy.

Princess Diana greets humans

- When requested what she did, Diana said, "I swam," bringing up that when she and Prince Charles had been on Australia and that they were greeting human beings, she had requested her husband what she become speculated to do. Prince Charles counseled her to go to the other element and speak to the human beings there. Left on her private, Diana did as informed.

By the surrender of the day, she located out that she must sort herself out. When they flew again to New Zealand, she said she become a unique person. She located out the texture of responsibility, the amount of hobby and the disturbing position she located herself in. Diana brought that she emerge as overwhelmed through the pressure from the human beings, announcing that being a princess changed right into a hard undertaking. And at 21 years antique, she couldn't apprehend the extent of interest that human beings had to her.

At first, Diana become harassed through manner of which location she want to move into. And then she decided herself involved and working with parents who have been rejected with the aid of the society, which consist of drug addicts and alcoholics. She in particular said how honest those human beings have been, especially the ones in hospices that she visited. Diana said that when people are death, they're greater open and willing and masses greater real than exceptional people. And this changed into one detail that she favored approximately her new characteristic as a princess.

Bashir asked her whether or not or not or now not the palace had given any idea to a role that she can also have. Diana said no, and that no man or woman sat her down together along with her listing of duties. She said that she modified into fortunate enough to have decided her role, and he or she or he cherished being with humans.

True enough, humans spherical the arena located a satisfied, actual Diana every time she met humans from particular global places. She wasn't afraid to mingle with human beings who've AIDS or one of a kind illness. In her interview with Bashir, she said humans had been stunned on the equal time as she sat in clinic beds and held humans's fingers because of the truth they have got in no way visible it in advance than. But for Diana, it have come to be a normal problem to do. And at the same time as she observed the assurance that such motion gave, she did it anywhere.

One unique event come to be the fall of 1981 while she determined Prince Charles on a tour of Wales. Unexpectedly, some of human beings regarded at a few degree within the visits, and this on my own become a easy indication that the people have been greater than satisfied with their new princess.

Although the majority of the people got here simply to appearance her, it changed into now not sincerely her appearance that stuck their hobby. It became clean that Diana has a gift for speakme to strangers as friends, overcoming the barrier with great a single remark or question. This actual hobby to the humans have become what would probable grow to be one in each of Diana's legacies.

Charity Work

In 1983, Princess Diana confided within the then-Premier of Newfoundland, Brian Peckford, that she decided it very hard to address being a princess, however she end up gaining knowledge of. From the mid-Eighties, Diana have turn out to be associated with numerous charities. She made public appearances to hospitals and colleges, among others. Her lively involvement made her the twentieth century version of royal patronage.

Princess Diana talks with the lots lots much less lucky human beings

- Over time, Princess Diana have end up plenty more interested by excessive ailments and distinct fitness-related topics which have been past the scope of traditional royal involvement. In specific, she had worked with AIDS and leprosy patients. She modified into moreover the patroness of charities and limitless agencies that labored with the homeless, kids, drug addicts and the elderly. But maximum of these charities and companies, mainly the primary ones that she supported, had to do with children.

- She worked with extra than one hundred charities at some point of her years as a princess, but she resigned to over 100 charities and centered with the closing six. Princess Diana's great achievement come to be turning into an global well-known determine of superb achievement and recognition. She has this characteristic that endeared humans to her, and her human touch become what linked her to the much much less lucky lives of those she met.

- What made Diana endearing to the public became the functionality to deal with all and sundry as equals. No extraordinary royal family member had reached out to the loads the way she did. And in spite of the truth that she may additionally furthermore have appeared shy, Diana's self-guarantee slowly emerged. By 1984, Diana's self-warranty in her public works modified into apparent. She have end up greater well-known, more so because of the intangible exquisite of care that extended her recognition above the expectations at the contributors of the Royal Family.

Princess Diana visits Dr Barnardo's Headquarters in 1985

- Diana supported endless charities and groups, tirelessly attending activities and lending her help to fund-elevating. And commonly with top notch effects. She have become president of the Royal Marsden Hospital and patron of the National Hospital for Neurology and Neurosurgery. She additionally have turn out to be client of Help the Aged and of the Guinness Trust.

- Diana did not overlook approximately helping charities that had to do with youngsters. In 1989 she have come to be consumer of the National Meningitis Trust and a one year later have grow to be the patron of the Hospital for Sick Children at

Great Ormond Street. It have emerge as in which she had rushed Prince William at the same time as he had an twist of destiny fracturing his cranium at college. The following year, she visited hostels for the homeless, and she additionally visited humans with AIDS. She met Mother Theresa on her 1992 adventure to Rome.

- After her separation with Prince Charles, Diana centered on her charity paintings, particularly to drug dependency clinics, marriage-steerage facilities and refuges for battered women. Diana in no way stopped running with charities that supported AIDS patients. She should consolation the dad and mom and can let each person recognise that they have to now not be handled as outcasts. She changed into prepared to shake fingers with patients with AIDS and leprosy. She modified attitudes.

- In 1991, Princess Diana and Barbara Bush, partner of the American president, visited the AIDS ward of the Middlesex Hospital in which she hugged a patient. This action emphasized her speech that she gave earlier in which she said,

"HIV does now not make humans dangerous to understand, so you can shake their arms and supply them a hug – heaven is privy to, they need it. What's more, you can percentage their homes, their places of work, and their playgrounds and toys."

Diana additionally campaigned in useful resource of leprosy sufferers. Way returned in 1989, she and Prince Charles visited Indonesia, in which she asked to go to the Sitanela Leprosy Hospital. Diana shook palms with patients, plenty of which have been children. In 1990, she visited a leper health facility in Nigeria. She would later emerge as a client of the Leprosy Mission in Britain. In September 1994, following her withdrawal from public life, Diana earned the name of International Humanitarian of the Year.

The Anti-Personnel Mine Ban Convention

The Anti-Personnel Mine Ban Convention, or the Ottawa Treaty, aimed to remove anti-employees landmines round the arena. Princess Diana emerge as a massive participant inside the formation technique of the Ottawa Treaty. In 1997, she paid Angola a go to as a guest of the International Red Cross and walked instances thru a minefield. During this year, the us's populace changed into approximately 10 million and the land mines have been approximately 10-20 million in area from its civil warfare. Later that identical one year, Princess Diana visited Bosnia with the Landmine Survivors Network.

Princess Diana tours a minefield

- Diana modified into diagnosed for her contributions as she centered at the accidents and deaths inflicted on kids. David Clark, shadow safety spokesman, stated that the people need to appreciate the reality that Princess Diana had long lengthy beyond to Angola and had tried to warn the area approximately the risks of anti-personnel landmines.

- It come to be noted that Princess Diana's involvement transformed the advertising and marketing campaign and taken pressure on governments to comply to a international ban. Her immoderate-profile journeys to Angola and Bosnia drew interest to the suffering of mine patients. Several critics, alongside aspect Conservative politicians, criticized her for straying into the political area and for being "a free cannon," "sick-recommended," and "now not useful or sensible" in her name to abolish the landmines.

- Diana have become very energetic in the International Campaign to Ban Landmines. It won a Nobel Peace Prize in 1997, only a few months after her lack of life. Despite the criticisms, human beings could continuously do not forget Diana's contributions to the advertising and marketing campaign, mainly the patients who subsequently had their voice heard thru Diana.

National AIDS Trust

Princess Diana made a big contribution to NAT and become a purchaser from 1991 to 1997. Her efforts added to the worldwide fight toward HIV and AIDS. Her willpower to elevate the profile of HIV helped to task the stigma of HIV virus across the area.

- Diana have emerge as extra famous for bravely shaking hands and speaking with AIDS sufferers. At a time while people despite the fact that believed that AIDS is probably surpassed spherical thru informal touch, Diana bravely sat at the health center mattress of someone with AIDS and held his hand. Diana's easy gesture showed the world that folks that suffered from AIDS did now not deserve isolation. Instead, they desired compassion. Diana modified into instrumental in changing global opinion, giving wish to human beings with AIDS, and growing recognition for the ones who have been at hazard.

- In February 1989, Diana visited and spent 3 days in New York all via herself. She visited the agreement middle inside the poverty-bothered Lower East Side. She specially went to the Aids unit inside the children's ward of Harlem Hospital and collected and hugged a seven-3 hundred and sixty 5 days-antique sufferer. Her spontaneous movement had the high-quality effect, for it created attention on a country that perceived the social unacceptability of AIDS.

The Queen of Hearts

Diana and Prince Charles' divorce confident that she had no possibilities of being a queen, but it gave Diana freedom, a few aspect that she turn out to be deprived due to the fact that her engagement. Somehow, Diana had stated of what lay in advance for her. A policeman had recommended her that night time time that she left her flat to stay at Clarence Hall,

"I in reality want you to recognize that that is your closing night time of freedom ever within the relaxation of your life. So make the most of it."

And for the rest of her married lifestyles, Diana felt trapped. Where she lived felt greater like a jail than a fort. But in choice to sulking, Diana concept of better use for her time. She occupied herself in conjunction with her charity works, and this became wherein she decided happiness and fulfillment.

- For many years, Princess Diana modified into an avid purchaser of countless charities and groups, specially running with children and the outcasts of the society. Every day, there might be photographs of Diana on newspapers and magazines hugging a small little one, or speakme with a few humans with a grin. Her harsh critics claimed it end up best for display, however Diana had changed lives forever.

Princess Diana touched the lives of many human beings

- Indeed, Diana's selflessness and being concerned for a bargain much less lucky humans have been developments that she exhibited in the course of her life. She might also additionally want to have used her fame and wealth to stay an extravagant existence. Instead, she used it to help others. She discovered out later that in her position as a princess, it end up some distance extra enjoyable to supply kindness to the the ones who've been handled unkindly and to help and supply want to the helpless and hopeless.

Chapter 10: The Marriage Breaks Down

There isn't any doubt that those who watched the royal bridal ceremony hoped that the marriage may additionally need to artwork. Prince Charles and Diana's tale changed into proper faraway from a fairy tale, and that they had been expected to "live luckily ever after." And on the identical time as inside the first months in their marriage Diana have grow to be happy as any bride can be, fast that happiness may be confronted via masses of things that threatened, and succeeded, to topple the marriage.

- People were effortlessly fooled with the aid of the grins and togetherness that they discovered of the royal couple. Princess Diana have end up generally via her husband's issue at the same time as travelling worldwide locations or at the same time as greeting human beings. They furnished a unified the front for the Royal Family. But, as Diana confided later, it changed into only a charade.

The Other Woman: Camilla Parker-Bowles

The couple had marital issues as early as 1985. Even in the path of their engagement, Diana had had the feeling that Charles' former lady friend, Camilla Parker-Bowles, became actually across the nook, exerting a effective role in Charles' lifestyles. In truth, it changed into to be decided out for the primary time for the duration of the name of the game taped interviews with Diana that on their wedding, she knew that Charles changed into despite the fact that concerned with Camilla, however she hoped that the relationship have become over.

Camilla Parker-Bowles

- On her wedding ceremony day, as Diana emerged the glass carriage, she felt like she emerge as going to an execution. She later on said that,

- "I have grow to be very, very deathly calm, deathly, deathly calm. I felt as despite the fact that I modified into…a lamb to the slaughter. And I knew it, however I couldn't perform a little element approximately it."

It was sincerely pomp and spectacle. There have been 3,500 guests inside the Cathedral, but she modified into seeking out absolutely one man or woman. She noticed Camilla together with her faded grey pillbox hat. But Diana modified into very a whole lot in love with Prince Charles, and she or he hoped that the relationship among her husband and Camilla modified into over.

- How wrong she modified into. From her engagement to her demise, there was constantly Camilla's shadow throughout the corner. And Diana have turn out to be very jealous, in particular at the same time as her suspicions were confirmed. Charles had decided the woman he favored in Camilla, a person who inspired his mind. He had generally felt that Camilla changed into a first rate confidante.

- Camilla and Prince Charles' dating started out out in 1970 when they met at a polo healthful. She changed into first-rate one of the prince's numerous girlfriends, however it have become said that he had preferred to marry her. However, royal courtiers perceived that Camilla come to be no longer an appropriate wholesome for Charles. Also, Charles had met Camilla too early. His Uncle Dickie have come to be allegedly to have Charles published distant places at the way to surrender his dating with Camilla.

- Reports mounted that the 2 rekindled their relationship in the past due 1970s and past due 1980s. Camilla married Andrew Parker-Bowles, an Army captain, in July 1973, however it modified into an unhappy marriage. Himself a womanizer, Parker-Bowles turn out to be stated to have diagnosed and gave entire consent to Camilla's courting with the prince at some stage in their marriage. This earned him the name because the "guy who laid down his companion for his usa."

Prince Charles and Camilla on their younger days

- In 1992, after the guide of Diana: Her True Story by the usage of Andrew Morton, Diana found the ones affairs. In November of the same 12 months, the Today and the Mirror newspapers published the transcript of the leaked "Camillagate" tapes, which had been the intimate exchanges amongst Prince Charles and Camilla.

- Diana had moreover found out that she overheard Charles speakme on the smartphone in his bathtub and he stated, "Whatever takes place, I'll continuously love you." She instructed him she listened on the door, and they had a combat.

A month after the engagement declaration, Charles left on a 5-week excursion of Australia, New Zealand, Venezuela and the USA. Diana changed into seen crying, but many folks that noticed her assumed she became already lacking her Prince. But it have become something else. Before Prince Charles left, the telephone rang and it come to be a call from Camilla. She left them to it, but it have become heartbreaking for her.

On their honeymoon, they had been starting their diaries to talk approximately topics at the same time as photographs of Camilla fell out from Prince Charles' diary. This have turn out to be each distinctive affirmation that he had actually resumed his courting together along with his former girl friend. And on a white tie dinner for President Sadat, Diana found that Prince Charles' cuff links have end up engraved with C's entwined. She stated,

"Camilla gave you the ones didn't she?"

Prince Charles replied, "Yes, so what's incorrect? They're a present from a friend." They had a row again, and Diana felt very jealous. Bulimia grow to be appalling, she stated. Sometimes she is probably sick four times on the yacht. She ate everything and could be unwell minutes later. This moreover accounted to her being very worn-out.

- On her interview with Martin Bashir in 1995, even as requested approximately Camilla, Diana said,

- "Well, there's three human beings in this marriage. So it's miles a piece crowded."

The love triangle

She have become powerless and jealous of Camilla, specifically at the same time as Prince Charles stopped sleeping together with his spouse after their 1987 journey to Portugal. Diana stated,

"Shop closed up proper away after Portugal. And that modified into it. And whether or not that meant that Camilla had come again in a large vengeance, I don't have any idea. I had no proof."

Bulimia and Suicide Attempts

Diana had suffered from bulimia because her engagement to Prince Charles. Diana also placed out quick enough that Prince Charles had although touch with Camilla, and this affected her health. In sincerely 5 months, she had out of area 5 and a half of inches in her waist, and that wouldn't look accurate on a marriage get dressed. Diana stated that bulimia started out out every week once they have been given engaged. She remembered her husband located his hand on her waistline and stated,

"Oh, a chunk overweight right proper right here, aren't we?"

It introduced on some element in Diana, who've come to be thrilled at the number one time she made herself sick due to the fact she concept it turned into a release from anxiety.

The illness end up some detail she had battled for years. She even had an episode of bulimia the night time earlier than her bridal ceremony while she determined a bracelet that Prince Charles was giving Camilla. She ate the whole lot that night time and she have become sick afterwards. Diana diagnosed that it modified into an instance of what changed into taking place.

- Diana's spirit have become so low and her sisters attempted to cheer her up. Diana said,

- "I can't marry him. I can't do that. This is definitely high-quality."

But Diana had no way of taking flight as it modified into too overdue and he or she had no way out. On the streets, there have been banners pronouncing the Royal nuptials.

A tea towel saying the royal wedding ceremony

- Her warfare with bulimia persisted even on their honeymoon. When she positioned out that Prince Charles' cuff hyperlinks with the 2 C's entwined came from Camilla, it drove her to episodes of bulimia. Of bulimia, Diana had said,

"I wasn't well in any respect. I informed anyone I turn out to be tired the complete time, however it come to be the bulimia that had genuinely taken grip of me."

Prince Charles couldn't care sufficient. On their 1986 journey to Canada, she fainted. She stated,

"My husband informed me off. He stated I need to have surpassed out quietly some location else within the returned of a door."

This incident have grow to be speedy picked up via the press, and they attributed it to warmness and fatigue.

- Five months into their marriage, within the New Year of 1985, Diana notion that Charles changed into incapable of knowledge what she became going through. She stated that she resorted to bulimia and to mutilating herself to get the eye of her husband, but Charles misunderstood her. Even the rest of the royal own family concept she changed into crying wolf to get hobby.

- Diana moreover devoted half-hearted attempts of suicide. There were several times at the identical time as she tried to reduce her wrists with razor blades, lemon knife and pen knife, however Charles, or anybody inside the Palace, did no longer take her critically. As normal, they thought she come to be simply crying wolf.

- At one time, Charles had said to her, "I'm not going to pay interest. You're always doing this to me. I'm going using now." Diana threw herself down the stairs, know-how she changed into pregnant. The Queen arrived and became horrified and frightened. Diana knew she wasn't going to lose the toddler, even though she emerge as bruised for the duration of the stomach. Charles went out riding. And while he came decrease lower back, it have grow to be as despite the fact that not anything took place. Dismissal, as Diana stated.

- During the mid-Nineteen Eighties, Diana all over again to London from Scotland in advance than deliberate. The media, also false impression Diana, said that she desired to buy groceries. The reality modified into that she modified into very unwell and the royal circle of relatives changed into maintaining it from the overall public. She had to come down for treatment because of the reality she have turn out to be searching for to reduce her wrists with razor blades.

- On one event, 5 years into her marriage, Diana's sister, Jane, paid her a visit and asked her about the markings on her chest which have become seen thru her V-neck. Diana recalled that the night time earlier than, she preferred to talk to Charles approximately some issue however he wouldn't be aware of her, saying she was crying wolf. Diana picked up his pen knife and scratched herself carefully down the chest and both thighs. There become some of blood however Charles did now not reacted.

- Diana become craving for a person, maximum particularly her husband, to recognize her. She said,

"I changed into honestly so decided. I knew what became wrong with me. But no character else round me understood me. I desired rest and to be looked after interior my residence and for human beings to understand the torment and the pain taking place in my head...I surely had to be allowed to comply to my new function."

Diana said that within the speak of the palace regarding her weight loss, the Queen herself spread the tale that Charles informed about her. "He in truth knowledgeable her about my bulimia and she or he knowledgeable every person that modified into the motive why our marriage had cracked up – due to the truth Diana's consuming need to be so tough for Charles."

Diana's Affairs

In the mid-1980s, Diana became to others for affection. She had numerous affairs with a few men at the same time as however married to Prince Charles, irrespective of the reality that some of her closest pals could in all likelihood attest that she began her affairs after Charles again to Camilla's arms. She grew to turn out to be to the ones men searching out some factor that she did not discover from her husband: to be sincerely cherished.

James Hewitt

Diana had an affair with James Hewitt that lasted 5 years. Some reviews indicated that the affair began in 1986 whilst the royal couple's marriage became within the new lows, whilst others claimed that it started out finally after Prince Harry's begin. Hewitt become a British own family cavalry officer inside the British Army whom Diana met at a mutual friend's night meal. They mentioned riding horses, and Diana stated she favored to overcome her worry of the usage of. He modified into able to be added as a capability trainer for her and her sons.

James Hewitt

- Hewitt said in an interview that he had no ulterior purpose other than to train her the way to journey. Princess Diana changed into married to Prince Charles, and Diana's hobby in him became due to her desire to get a horse the usage of instructor for her children. It become a professional undertaking, Hewitt said, and it turn out to be fast organized with the useful resource of Diana's woman-in-geared up to go back and experience from the backs. She got here to adventure and to break out the pressures of her ordinary each day recurring.

- Diana had no person to turn to, and Hewitt changed into there to pay attention. In 1986, it become becoming obvious that the royal couple's fairy tale marriage turned into beginning to fail. Rumors had abounded approximately the developing rift a few of the royal couple. And Hewitt changed into continuously there, being sympathetic to Diana proper from the start. According to Andrew Morton, her dating with Hewitt helped her regain a revel in of vanity.

- But their courting grow to be now not supposed to flourish. They were no longer intellectually well matched, and Hewitt was additionally stationed in Germany within the past due Nineteen Eighties to feature chief of a tank squadron. They tried to re-light their dating after Hewitt decrease returned from Germany, but he turn out to be then despatched away to the Persian Gulf in 1991. Diana mailed him passionate letters, every now and then four in a day, telling him how she longed for him and the way upset she turn out to be that she remained in her marriage.

- Their courting have end up public in the direction of the Gulf War at the identical time as Hewitt's estranged woman buddy, Emma Stewardson determined to the News of the World that Diana emerge as sending him gadgets and love letters. There come to be no mention of a sexual dating, however the media reviews absolutely worried Diana to three diploma. It became her husband's infidelities that she preferred publicized and not her very personal.

- Upon Hewitt's skip lower returned from the Gulf War, he visited Diana at Highgrove. They have been careful no longer to be visible through using manner of the press, and so Hewitt needed to hide within the trunk of the auto on his manner to appearance her. Diana changed into also scared that greater humans will suspect her reference to Hewitt, and so she slowly distanced herself from Hewitt.

James Gilbey

James Gilbey changed into a teens buddy whom Diana whilst she changed into 17. In 1989, at the same time as Hewitt left for Germany, Diana began out out a relationship with Gilbey. At first, they pointed out their love lives that had long past awry, after which it blossomed proper right into a romance. Gilbey affectionately known as Diana "Squidgy," and their leaked intimate taped mobile phone communication that have been given into the hands of the media modified into dubbed "Squidgygate." This conversation befell on New Year's Eve of 1989 in which they pointed out their emotions for every other.

James Gilbey

- Although their relationship flourished in 1989, Diana despite the reality that longed for Hewitt. She did not experience passionate about Gilbey the way he modified into along with her. She desired Gilbey, however he referred to as her "darling" 14 times and as "Squidgy" or "Squidge" fifty three times all during their communication.

- It became throughout this taped communique that Diana confided in Gilbey approximately her courting with the royal circle of relatives and how she turn out to be overcome thru sadness. She furthermore informed him that she felt restricted with the beneficial aid of the confines of her marriage, and that Charles made her lifestyles "actual torture."

Prince Charles' Lack of Love

Diana could not be blamed if she favored to fill an emotional void. She loved Charles, and regardless of the telltale signs and signs and symptoms of marital troubles, she although hoped that their marriage may be salvaged regardless of their sexual encounters with others. But Charles' lack of affection haunted Diana.

Prince Charles found out in an interview that he in no way cherished Diana

- When they had been collectively, which have been becoming seldom, they might commonly have horrible fights. Palace body of workers ought to pay attention raised voices, slammed doors, then silence. At times the fights had been violent. Their families urged Diana to restore her relationship with Charles, but the marriage turned into beyond restore. Any probabilities of reconciliation best ended up in greater fights and accusations.

- Diana's personal bodyguard, who knew approximately her love lifestyles, attested that Diana's having her non-public affairs with a few guys became a protest, greater like announcing to Charles, "If you may do this, so can I."

- There changed into moreover one incident in 1990, really after Prince William grew to come to be 8, while Charles broke his arm whilst he tumbled off his polo pony. He became taken to the Queen's Medical Centre in Nottingham for surgical remedy. Diana end up first-rate too glad to take the possibility to select him up from the medical institution and bring him home in which she have to nurse him decrease lower returned to health. But Charles rejected her and knowledgeable her that he favored to be left on my own. Diana drove once more to London in tears while Camilla arrived at Highgrove to be with Charles. Paul Burrel, the royal butler, recalled how glad Charles changed into upon seeing Camilla.

- Although they have been despite the fact that together interior the feel that no separation or divorce became in movement, the couple not often noticed each different except on the identical time as wearing out royal responsibilities. Paul Burrell witnessed that the connection among Prince Charles and Princess Diana changed into reduced to in fact being business enterprise friends. On their trips abroad, they may stay in separate rooms or maybe separate flooring. Burrell said that Diana not had feelings for her husband, and he or she become bored to death with the stern protocol that modified into required of her as a princess.

- It have turn out to be moreover cited how Prince Charles might harshly criticize Diana's appearance and performance. He took every possibility to insult her flavor of apparel. For example, on their journey to Czechoslovakia in 1991, Diana had worn a black-and-white variety for a day occasion. In the the front of the attending officials, Charles commented,

- "You seem like you've sincerely joined the Mafia."

It have turn out to be now not funny, however he succeeded in humiliating his spouse inside the the front of others. This delivered to Diana's lack of self assurance. In the decision of the sport taped interviews, she stated,

"I hated myself plenty. I didn't suppose I turned into real enough. I concept that I wasn't suitable sufficient for Charles…My husband made me revel in so insufficient in each viable way, that every time I got here up for air he pushed me down over again."

Also, Diana became more famous than Charles, and this changed into an embarrassment to him. After all, Diana did not come from a royal family, and but it grow to be she who constantly graced the covers of magazines and newspapers. The media's interest in her fantastic served to irk Prince Charles.

The Last Straw

For the primary time in 1991, Diana started to take manipulate of her existence. She positioned new electricity and self perception following her war of words of Camilla on the latter's sister's birthday celebration wherein Diana informed her that she knew approximately the affair. Diana said she turned into not pleased but she became a excellent deal happier and content material fabric fabric than she had ever been.

- In getting prepared her for a separation from Prince Charles that could not have an impact on her reputation as a princess, monetary adviser Joseph Sanders and Diana's antique pal and adviser Dr. James Colthurst determined to have a e-book written about Diana's existence. The e-book may be written with the aid of manner of freelance creator Andrew Morton, Colthurst's buddy, who had previously written newspaper articles approximately the royal family.

- Diana made her boldest flow into but to show her mystery misery to the sector. But telling the sort of story that she had in mind may harm the rules of royal behavior. And so she have to stay anonymous as she feared the outcomes of what she emerge as about to do. The royal circle of relatives has the power to pronounce her mentally unsound or worse. Colthurst stated in an interview that the monarch had manipulate over Diana's kids, and she or he grow to be aware of this. She become concerned that she ought to lose the youngsters.

Andrew Morton

- Andrew Morton, Michael O'Mara the writer and Colthurst must defend Diana as she changed into carefully watched by using way of photographers and palace frame of people. And in order that they devised a plan. Morton wrote questions for Diana and gave them to Colthurst, who was already a regular traveler to Diana's residence. Colthurst could possibly go to Kensington Palace bringing with him a tape recorder, and would depart the palace with the recorded answers of Diana to Morton's questions. All in all there were 6 tapes.

- The revelations from those tapes were so damning that O'Mara feared the consequences if the writing scheme emerge as placed. Morton ought to likely effortlessly turn out to be in court docket docket. They took greater precautions and had their workplaces swept for bugs. Morton's place of work come to be burgled and ransacked. For nearly 6 months, with every new financial catastrophe, they've become greater anxious.

The e-book on Diana's existence

- The Sunday Times serialized Morton's ebook beginning June 7, 1992. The public couldn't agree with what they check on the newspaper. Most importantly, the palace changed into bowled over and caught truly off-protect via the object. According to royal biographer Penny Junor,

"I assume the Queen come to be livid. There's not a family inside the global, I assume, that might want to look the marital issues broadcast everywhere inside the global."

The reaction have become a few aspect that Diana, Morton and Colthurst want to have imagined. The conspirators attempted to cover the fact that Diana have become the source of the substances.

- The days following the serialization of the ebook had been packed with uncertainty. Diana become fearful and had 2nd thoughts. Although rival guides attempted to plant doubts approximately the authenticity of the information, their efforts failed.

- As the excerpts of the ebook endured to be serialized, it have come to be apparent that Diana had contributed appreciably to its content cloth. This have become further cemented even as the media noticed Diana collectively along with her pal Bartholomew who become interviewed for the ebook. Those who felt deceived with the useful resource of the usage of Diana whilst she said she did not have a few issue to do with the ebook have been indignant together with her.

- Also, the humans of the British press criticized Morton and the Sunday Times, and their reaction modified into precipitated via way of manner of a code of British newshounds that the royal family is sacred. Some might even circulate as far as to say that Morton cared for the coins in choice to within the survival of the royal own family. But nevertheless first-rate people did not accept as true with that Diana collaborated with Morton for the ebook.

- But quickly enough, it became easy that the click and the people supported her. Letters started to achieve from the general public, prompting her to recognize that she hadn't devoted a large sin.

- The royal own family, left to lick their very personal wounds, emerge as stunned through the usage of the turn of sports. Charles had spoken to the Queen about placing apart from Diana but he grow to be knowledgeable to endure it for six months. But the revelations in Morton's books delivered approximately the royal family to preserve with the separation in advance. They made it smooth that Prince Charles' infidelity became not anything in comparison to the notions of criticizing and revealing secrets and techniques about the royal own family.

- Diana have become called to meet with the Queen and Prince Philip at Windsor Castle the day earlier than the ebook have turn out to be to be published. She though denied her involvement within the ebook, and she refused to apologize for what she did. She advised them how a super deal she hated Camilla and that she wanted a trial separation. For years she stored to herself her feelings about Charles, his mistress and her dating with the royal circle of relatives. But now she modified into more comfortable as she have end up in a function to tell the Queen and Prince Philip about the ones topics.

- Shortly thereafter, tabloids posted the Squidgygate tapes, that have been a recording of a conversation amongst Gilbey and Diana, and a Sun article said that Diana had maintained her dating with Hewitt. Diana released a lawsuit towards the Sun but she did now not deliver it to court docket. Close pals of Diana made it recognized how the terrible press damage the princess.

The Squidgygate emerge as a telephone communique among Gilbey and Princess Diana

- The Camillagate tapes speedy surfaced. The tapes have been recordings of a totally intimate and sexually explicit communique amongst Prince Charles and Camilla. This confirmed Charles' infidelity and brought into query his suitability to be king.

- In November, Charles and Diana argued over which of them have to go together with William and Harry on the weekend of November 19. It come to be assumed that the kids have to go along with their father to a taking pictures party, however Diana had moreover take into account to spend time collectively along side her children by myself because of the reality she could not undergo to be round her husband. Charles have been given irritated and recommended Diana of his choice for a separation.

Chapter 11: The Princess' Life After The Separation

A terrific weight grow to be lifted off Diana's shoulders on the same time as she and Prince Charles separated. By this time, she became very rich, well-known, cherished through people and on her very own. Although she end up despite the fact that beneath the scrutiny of the media and the palace frame of people, in some manner, lifestyles turn out to be extra bearable, and she have become taking care of her youngsters. Only 31 years vintage, Diana knew it have become now not too late to study what existence needed to provide for her.

- Quite all at once, the overall public sympathized with Diana, but this got here no longer as a surprise for all because of the fact Diana was commonly the fave in Britain and spherical the sector, specifically amongst women. Just a month earlier, the entire transcription of the Camillagate tapes have been posted, and Diana's image as a victim of Charles' infidelity changed into set up. Even with all the facts regarding Diana's very personal affairs with Hewitt and other men, Charles' sexually-charged verbal exchange with Camilla confirmed that it have turn out to be he who entered into an affair first.

Independent Woman

All that Diana had been via while married to Prince Charles made her a robust and impartial girl. Despite the ache from a loveless marriage and the stigma of bulimia, she knew she had to go with the flow on. She come to be indeed a extraordinary woman.

- Following the separation, Diana introduced that she became retreating from public lifestyles on December three, 1993. She stated that she wanted time and space for every herself and her sons. She resigned to extra than 100 charities that she supported so she want to awareness on six.

- Although she renounced public responsibilities, Diana placed it no longer feasible to live out of the overall public spotlight. In 1994, she posed for Vogue which published her glamorous photographs. This have become placed with the useful resource of newspaper evaluations revealing her dating with James Hewitt. He admitted to having a sexual courting with Diana. But in advance than Diana have to lick her wounds, a tv documentary in June 1994 showed Prince Charles admitting that he committed adultery.

Diana posed for Vogue magazine

- As each of them admitted to infidelity, the damage to Prince Charles became a protracted way greater. One difficulty became attributed to the truth that Charles have become raised inside the royal own family, some other modified into the truth that he participated in such sexually oriented communique that in addition destroyed his choice to be taken extensively. He had desired to gain admire for his political opinions, however his fable of being have become a tampon should not deliver him that recognize.

- Diana got here unscathed from all of the awful press approximately her. It modified into stated that her infidelities were not showed. People sided collectively together with her, being the victim of Charles' unfaithfulness. Women understood her and stated that Diana have grow to be a image of woman victimization. Diana took it all in gladly. She felt that she changed into not chained to her every day ordinary that got here with being a member of the royal family. She have become unfastened.

- Other disturbing situations grow to be inside the path of Diana as she tried to live a lifestyles that modified into definitely extraordinary than the only she had lived whilst she changed into despite the reality that tied to Prince Charles. For example, newspapers wrote articles about Diana pestering Oliver Hoare, a close friend of her and Prince Charles, whom she had an affair with. And then there has been Hewitt, who end up seeking to coins in on his affair with Diana. Hewitt desperately favored the coins, and numerous tabloids and publishers were inclined to pay him for his story. He even met with journalist Diana Pasternak, who posted a e-book titled Princess in Love.

- Princess Diana modified into frightened at the equal time because the e-book hit the shelves. But Diana have come to be able to breathe deeply, seeing the October eight,

1994 headline of the Daily Mirror saying that she become not to be blamed for her moves. There end up a ballot in the newspaper which placed that first-class 27 of the readers blamed Diana for her affair with James Hewitt. There modified into a trifling 15 percent who said that their opinion of Diana have become stained. Surprisingly, extra than 80 percent pointed to Charles because the most effective detail that drove Diana into having an affair, and 61 percentage notion that the couple ought to divorce proper now. Seventy-three percentage of the readers believed that Queen Elizabeth II have to be the last British monarch.

- In March 1994, British tv character consider to create a documentary and a biography approximately Prince Charles. The televised documentary changed into first-class remembered for the detail wherein Prince Charles admitted to committing adultery at the same time as married to Diana. He emphasised that he had lengthy lengthy long gone off beam great whilst he believed that the marriage modified into irretrievably useless.

Princess Diana sporting the famous black get dressed

- Diana became now not capable to have a look at the documentary due to the fact that night time, she attended a fund-elevating dinner carrying a attractive black dress that stole the spotlight. Diana decided that humans in Britain and throughout the arena nonetheless loved her. Diana changed into free to be herself, and she or he took solo flights to Zimbabwe and Nepal. She changed into more of a British ambassador. She concerned herself with the International Red Cross and labored to further growth attention of AIDS and poverty.

- Sadly, Diana modified into nevertheless not over Charles. Although it changed into already years on account that their separation and he or she or he had relationships with unique guys, she turn out to be nonetheless irritated at Charles. She modified into angrier at the same time as he admitted within the interview with Dimbleby that he in no way cherished Diana from the begin. Diana said to a chum,

"Making that declaration confirmed what a egocentric prig Charles had become, as despite the fact that now not something in the international subjects, besides his feelings – no longer his wife, his kids, or any in their memories. I must gladly have scratched his eyes out for announcing that to the world."

The Panorama Interview

Later on, Diana modified into known as in a meeting with Queen Elizabeth II and Prince Philip. They admonished her for her extremely-modern behavior, even threatening that she be stripped of her call if her conduct did not beautify. This changed into in light of Diana's relationship with Will Carling, a hunky and without a doubt a tremendous deal married British rugby famous man or woman. He became her unofficial private teacher.

- Though Diana or Will did no longer admit that theirs end up a sexual relationship, a number of guides have claimed that it turn out to be of a sexual nature. And Carling's spouse, Julia, made it identified that Diana have emerge as destroying the wedding. Will promised in no manner to look Diana again, but he become photographed at Kensington Palace turning in rugby shirts for William and Harry. The Carlings announced their separation swiftly after.

- Diana insisted that her relationship with Will Carling become strictly platonic. In her preference to restore her reputation, Diana planned a inform-all interview with Martin Bashir on Panorama. The interview ran on

November 14, 1995, which coincidently became Prince Charles' forty seventh birthday. She wore a placing black eye makeup and noted her existence as a princess, her marriage, her youngsters, Camilla and a group of various things. There turn out to be an anticipated 23 million British visitors that day, which became taken into consideration the biggest target audience for any television documentary within the history of broadcasting.

Princess Diana with Martin Bashir

- Diana sturdy doubt to Prince Charles' functionality to guide the us as king, however she additionally made it stated approximately her non-public destiny function. She stated,

"I would really like to be a Queen in people's hearts...someone's were given to exit there and love humans."

- The Buckingham Palace have become again caught off defend with the resource of the interview. In it, Diana accused the royal family for no longer permitting her to develop as someone, for no longer crediting her performance, and for undermining her role as Princess of Wales after the separation. Diana said,

"Nobody ever helped me the least bit. They'd be there to criticize, however by no means be there to mention nicely finished."

Although the royal family and Diana's mom took it badly, the overall public had a incredible opinion. The Daily Mirror posted an opinion ballot which confirmed that 92 percentage of the respondents had been in manual of Diana's statements at a few degree inside the interview. Another ballot that the Sunday Times finished determined that -thirds of the British public authorised of the interview.

Divorce

One extraordinary incident sooner or later after the interview changed into Diana's war of words of Tiggy Legge-Bourke, the nanny that Prince Charles hired to appearance after William and Harry at the identical time as Diana emerge as away. The war of words passed off at a Christmas lunch upon her go back from New York. By then, Diana end up suspecting that Legge-Bourke turn out to be greater than an aide to Prince Charles.

- Diana approached the nanny and said,

- "Hello, Tiggy. How are you?...So sorry to pay attention about the little one."

Diana modified into speaking about Tiggy pregnancy through the Prince and having an abortion. Legge-Bourke left the room humiliated. She had contacted her legal professionals to trouble a statement that denied the allegations. It turn out to be moreover the final straw for the royal family of their elegance of Diana as a part of the own family.

A photograph showing Tiggy Legge-Bourke with Prince William, Prince Harry, and Prince Charles

- An research confirmed that Legge-Bourke visited her gynecologist two instances in 1995 however there was no proof that Legge-Bourke had an abortion. Diana refused to apologize. Charles and Queen Elizabeth had been delivered directly to insist on a hastened divorce.

- Weeks after the broadcast of the interview, the Queen sent letters to each Diana and Prince Charles urging them to divorce the soonest possible time. Diana obtained the letter from the Queen on December 18, 1995. Diana had complained to Paul Burrell that the queen approached Prime Minister John Major and the archbishop of Canterbury about the trouble earlier than drawing near her via a letter.

- On February 15, 1996, Diana had a assembly with the Queen in Buckingham

Palace. Diana still cared approximately Charles, and she or he or he requested the Queen whether or now not the prince need to marry Camilla. The Queen stated it end up not probable. Diana then said that she still cherished Charles and that she did now not want the divorce.

- Among the provisions of the divorce modified into that Diana's pick out is probably "Diana, Princess of Wales." The agreement furthermore gave Diana $2.2 million in a lump sum and about $six hundred,000 each three hundred and sixty five days to run her workplace. She changed into still a member of the royal family. On August 28, the wedding grow to be officially dissolved.

- It modified into simplest while the divorce became final that Diana felt free from an sad marriage and from the yoke of royalty. The unhappy financial ruin of her lifestyles became closed, however she had lots desire for what lay in advance for her now that she changed into a loose female. The years of charade ended, and now she can be herself.

Relationship With the Royal Family

Diana's relationship with the members of the royal own family come to be a piece strained. Although she stated that she have come to be in speaking terms with the Queen and the Duke of Edinburgh, it might not be to the issue of inviting them for tea. But Diana identified that the queen and Prince Philip exerted efforts to salvage her and Prince Charles' marriage.

- After the divorce have become very last, the royal own family need to have had to not listen anymore approximately Diana. The identical Queen who regular her into the own family have emerge as the identical person who rejected her after the separation. As it grew to turn out to be out, Diana have emerge as as famous as ever and persevered to upstage the royal own family as the clicking have become more interested by her.

- This modified into one difficulty that stained Diana's relationship with the royal family from the start or even after her loss of lifestyles. During the interview with Bashir in 1995, Diana admitted that she have become a happy female at some point of the early part of her marriage. She said that the stress on them as a couple with the media became out of the normal and misunderstood via a number of humans.

- As they walked spherical greeting human beings on their experience to Australia in some unspecified time in the future of the early years of marriage, Diana recalled how the people would possibly say, "Oh, she's on the opposite aspect." The royal family who took those authentic trips heard the same component for weeks, and it wasn't encouraging particularly for a proud guy like Prince Charles because it approach that the human beings came as much as appearance

Princess Diana. She stated that in choice to feeling happy, she felt low.

- In addition, Diana felt that the royal circle of relatives failed to recognize all her efforts not excellent for her circle of relatives however for the united states of the usa as an entire. They have in no way given her credit score score in a way that no character said 'Well accomplished' for something right she did however they got here down tough on her for every mistake she committed. It changed into tough for Diana to cope with this, and so she suffered bulimia as a way of break out.

Body language speaks louder than terms

- Diana moreover knowledgeable Bashir that the humans's choice for her became an uncomfortable depend to cope with. She felt it changed into unfair because of the reality she favored the attention for her husband. In fact, she modified into no longer flattered with the aid of the media interest as it brilliant ended to jealousy and complicated situations arose due to it.

- The royal family must have resented Diana's popularity some of the people. They have to have seen it as a hazard to their very own recognition. In the mid-1980s, Diana have turn out to be the style icon of Great Britain. People were very involved to look what she may want to located on, her hairdo, and her jewelries. People could scramble to get Diana's haircut, or discover a get dressed that carefully resembled Diana's cutting-edge outfit. Even the maximum mundane problem count, as prolonged as it had whatever to do with Diana, modified into observe with pretty an hobby from the human beings.

- In turn, Charles and the other individuals of the royal family were within the inner pages of the newspapers while pics of Diana graced the the front covers. Diana may additionally moreover have no longer been privy to strategies she upstaged Prince

Charles, but it damage him a wonderful deal. He had labored difficult to be well worth of his identify and when he have been given married, hit end up expected that Diana may also want to decrease lower back him up in his duties. But he best ended up being upstaged.

In reality, in the course of the 1984 State Opening of Parliament, Diana delivered approximately offence via growing a glamorous appearance with a totally new hairdo that confirmed her neck. The press couldn't help noticing how the human beings of the parliament goggled. Without a doubt, Charles appeared unhappy and the Queen became stated to be furious by using the use of manner of the display of showbiz-fashion glamor.

Princess Diana, Prince Charles and Queen Elizabeth II for the duration of the 1984 State Opening of Parliament

The next day, the newspapers' front cowl come to be a image of Diana together along with her new hairdo, and Queen Elizabeth II turned into inside the internal pages. The courses which have been purported to be committed to the royal own family centered on Diana and her youngsters. And as Diana located out that the media paid interest to her fabric cabinet, she commenced visiting with hundreds of outfits.

When Prince Charles and Princess Diana traveled to the united states, it modified into stated that Diana have come to be the dominant determine in the courting. In the October 1985 trouble of Vanity Fair, Tina Brown penned a chunk of writing titled "The Mouse That Roared" wherein she claimed that Diana had Charles below her thumb. She added that Diana's upward thrust to stardom had horrific outcomes on her and that Charles become vintage and dull past his years.

Diana's dating with the royal family after her prison separation with Prince Charles have come to be even extra hard. She modified into seen as a trouble and a felony responsibility with the resource of the people around her, even the royal own family. Diana stated that her visits remote places have been blocked, her letters were given out of place and that her obligations were held from her.

For instance, Diana expressed a choice to visit British troops and refugees in Bosnia, the Palace informed her that Prince Charles' plans to move there would be prioritized. And in September 1993, Diana turned into cautioned that she could not go to the Irish president in Dublin because of 'safety reasons.' This changed into obviously executed to resurrect the prince's public photo on the rate of reducing the recognition of Diana as princess. Diana suspected that the Establishment prevented her from playing a immoderate public profile that overshadowed Prince Charles.

She very an awful lot subtly hinted that her husband's department needed to do with the tape of her intimate verbal exchange with Gilbey leaking to the clicking. "It have grow to be carried out to harm me in a excessive manner," she said to Bashir, including that the movement emerge as meant to purpose the general public to alternate their attitudes in the route of Diana.

They had more troubles as Diana did not plan to move quietly. She need to combat to the prevent, however it come to be surprising whilst she delivered that she would probable withdraw from public lifestyles. Diana stated that the enemy – her husband's element – changed into amazed and stressed whilst she made the announcement. It changed into out of jealousy and worry that they desired to undermine her due to the reality Diana became greater famous and her art work turn out to be cited more than Charles.

Relationship With The Paparazzi

From the instantaneous the click heard about Prince Charles being in love yet again, Diana have grow to be a press obsession and were found with the aid of the usage of freelance photojournalists called the paparazzi. Partly, the media changed into chargeable for the developing reputation of Diana in Britain and the entire international. She changed into an exciting determine, diagnosed for her fashionable garments, beauty, and countless charity works. She have become extra famous than every one-of-a-kind member of the royal circle of relatives, and she or he became constantly observed by the usage of way of photographers everywhere she went. In reality, Diana have end up the maximum photographed woman within the international.

- Diana before the whole thing end up overwhelmed through the hobby that the media confirmed in her. She become now not used to the eye and she or he or he or he had a hard time with the click, along side that "that that they had truly haunted me, or hunted me." The press can also need to hound her for the relaxation of her lifestyles.

Princess Diana have end up hounded thru the press at the same time as you consider that her engagement with Prince Charles

- It need to were difficult for Diana to take it all in. From obscurity, she grow to be catapulted into reputation, and with that, the lack of privacy that she so loved earlier than meeting Prince Charles. What she did, everywhere she went, and all of the subjects approximately her have become stated to the area. Any photo possibility should pressure income through the roof, and so the paparazzi could take each opportunity to snap pics of the princess.

- Even even as she have been given pregnant, it modified into all of the greater interesting for the paparazzi. Some observed the royal couple as they went to Bahamas Island for tour in February 1982 and published images of Diana carrying a bikini in British papers. The photos have been interested in out the understanding or consent of the princess.

- Even earlier than Diana got here, the royal family had an prolonged information of a difficult dating with the clicking. They have commonly been the target for the paparazzi however the Queen's caution to the newspapers not to post personal photographs of the royal family. Since Diana's loss of life, the royal family have come to be a good buy extra vocal about criticizing the media. As a give up end result, the click were the scenario of a more excessive scrutiny.

- In the beyond, the paparazzi would possibly scout Sandringham and Balmoral to try and draw near photographs of the royal own family. The Telegraph claimed that based totally from the snap shots taken by means of the use of the paparazzi, the royal family turn out to be cruel to animals. According to the paper, there had been photographs of the Queen wringing the neck of a wounded pheasant and of the Earl of Wessex elevating a shepherd's crook to a canine in the path of a shoot. Prince Charles' spokesman said that the royal own family turned into entitled to privateness at some point of each day private sports activities.

- But this emerge as not the case for Princess Diana who claimed she modified into burdened. Her relationship with the press became complex. Her revelations of her relationship with Prince Charles and other damning facts approximately the royal family within the direction of the 1995 Panorama interview have been unheard of, and her admission of bulimia and half of of-hearted attempts to kill herself indeed ruffled feathers in the royal own family. But it have emerge as her loss of lifestyles in a automobile crash that became the lens to the paparazzi themselves who've been chasing the princess.

Too an lousy lot hobby given to Princess Diana modified into simply an excessive amount of for her

- Diana additionally stated that the media attention affected her marriage in any such manner that it made their marriage hard. She did now not want to hog all the attention. In reality, she wanted the media to portray them as a set running collectively. Unfortunately, the first rate media interest on her drove Charles to determine to do separate engagements. Diana regretted this because she preferred the commercial enterprise organisation of Charles.

- During the 1995 interview with Bashir, Diana stated that the maximum overwhelming factor of her being a princess have become the media hobby. The Palace recommended her and Prince Charles that after they were given engaged, the media may want to pass quietly, however it did now not. And once they have been married, they have been advised that the media could go with the flow quietly. Again, this did now not show up. The press suddenly started out out that specialize in her, and her pics could be at the the front net internet page of each newspaper each day. She was quoted as announcing,

- "The better the media placed you, area you, is the bigger the drop."

Diana modified into very loads aware about this, and she or he or he or he located out the manner to govern the clicking. She though positioned the hobby in her thru the click more unique, but she despite the fact that did not like the attention she were given. She knew that after doing her public duties as a princess, she is probably photographed. But afterwards, she changed into photographed every time she stepped out of her door.

- Her view of the media changed after being within the limelight within the direction of her years as the Princess of Wales. Although she did no longer get used to it, she knew that a ordinary day might advise being located through 4 vehicles, after which getting decrease once more to her car with approximately six paparazzi looking for to snap pix of her. She stated that the media nonetheless placed her after 15 years as a product that sells well.

- Some humans accused that Diana recommended the media, a few issue that Diana disagreed with. She knew that her dating with the press had long past a bargain extra difficult in that the clicking have become abusive and continuously pressured her. But Diana knew better than to allow the paparazzi wreck her day. She used them, and they used her.

- In her interview with Bashir, she stated that the media can be a exquisite deal greater of help in representing the u . S . A . Abroad. Diana stated,

"As I in reality have all this media hobby, permit's not virtually sit on this u . S . And be battered with the resource of way of it. Let's take them, these humans, out to symbolize this u.S. And the great functions of it foreign places."

Diana went on to mention that each time she went foreign places, there were 60 to 90 photographers from the UK that went collectively with her. She said that the media can be applied in a effective way to help the u . S ..

Search For Love

There have grow to be one difficulty that Prince Charles in no way gave Diana, and that become to be cherished. Growing up in a circle of relatives that had its proportion of americaand downs, and divorce, too,

Diana had wanted her marriage to artwork notwithstanding the differences among her and Charles. She had affairs with a few guys on the equal time as but married to the prince in her are seeking for of a person to provide her love, to appearance after her, and to lend an ear to her woes.

Hasnat Khan

Khan modified right into a coronary coronary heart and lung healthcare expert at Harefield Hospital London whilst Diana met him in the overdue 1995 at the Royal Brompton Hospital wherein she had visited a pal improving from coronary heart surgical operation. They had a discreet affair for two years which lasted only a few months in advance than her twist of destiny in 1997.

Princess Diana and Hasnat Khan

- Many of Diana's near pals attested that Khan have become the 'love of her life' and that she changed into dissatisfied while he ended their dating. She had favored to marry him. Khan seemingly broke up together collectively with her saying that he could not marry her due to their cultural differences as Khan changed into a Muslim. He moreover notion that marriage among them is probably doomed to failure.

- One of Diana's depended on pals, Rosa Monckton, claimed that Diana had no plans of marrying Dodi Fayed, Diana's boyfriend who moreover died at the twist of fate she have become in, because of the truth she became despite the fact that in love with Khan. So a brilliant deal in fact that she became inclined to convert to Islam in case you want to marry him. But she brushed off the concept even as Khan permit her apprehend that their dating couldn't artwork in the long time.

Dodi Fayed

Fayed changed into an Egyptian movie manufacturer, the son of billionaire Mohamed Al-Fayed, who used to very very

very own the Harrods branch preserve and owner of Fulham Football Club and the Hotel Ritz Paris.

- He and Diana commenced a specially publicized relationship in July 1997 hastily after Diana's breakup with Khan and Dodi's breakup with American model Kelly Fisher. Diana and Dodi first met about 10 years in the beyond even as he done with Prince Charles in a polo healthful, and all over again at the identical time as Diana and her sons have been touring in Mohamed Fayed's villa at St. Tropez.

- Dodi, known as a playboy, end up certainly an not going suitor for Diana. He lived a lifestyles complete of luxuries considering that he become born, and Diana changed into looking for to strip away the glamor of royalty. But Diana grow to be drawn to Dodi, who suffered with the loss of his mom and one in all a type close to cherished ones. Some people determined that Dodi has developments which have been in common with Prince Charles', consisting of their love for polo and the need to gain approval of their dominating fathers.

Princess Diana collectively together with her lover, Dodi Fayed

- The instances after they met have been considerably ripe for a brand new romance for Diana, whose animosity in the course of Camilla had tired and her dating with Charles superior and her public lifestyles had a modern-day path and success. Diana become starting to locate internal peace, and the time for the right man to go into her life in the long run arrived.

Chapter 12: The Death Of The Princess Of Hearts

The Accident

Diana and Dodi simply got here decrease again from their 9-day holiday on board Fayed's yacht the Jonikal and stopped in Paris, France en route to London. When they arrived at Le Bourget airport on that Saturday afternoon, a number of eager paparazzi had been looking in advance to along facet the drivers and protection guys from the Ritz lodge that Dodi's father owned.

- On their manner to the lodge, they stopped at what have emerge as as soon as the home of the Duke and Duchess of Windsor and Dodi confirmed Diana across the restored mansion. On their journey, they had been determined by means of way of manner of a few photographers using motorcycles and searching for to capture images of the couple. Dodi's bodyguard, Kes Wingfield, who modified into visiting in a lower decrease back-up protection automobile with Henri Paul, end up worried that a number of the cameramen can also fall and harm themselves.

- At 6:30 within the nighttime, Dodi left for the jewelry save of Alberto Repossi which Diana and Dodi visited a long at the same time as inside the beyond and wherein Diana determined a hoop that she favored. Dodi picked up the hoop and taken it to his condo. The couple had deliberate to go to Dodi's condominium in advance than having supper at Le BenoIt restaurant later within the night time time. Some of the couple's buddies recommended the opportunity that Dodi changed into to advise to Diana that night time.

- A little after 7, Diana and Dodi traveled to the latter's rental wherein they stayed for some hours. The paparazzi had snapped pictures of the couple popping out of Hotel Ritz and entering Dodi's apartment. They cancelled their eating place reserving because of the numerous paparazzi strolling after them and determined to move once more to the Ritz for dinner.

- They arrived at the resort at nine:50 inside the midnight, however then left for the Imperial Suite. At approximately the same time, Henri Paul, the deputy head of safety of Hotel Ritz, turn out to be assigned to force the Mercedes which may take the couple lower back to Dodi's condominium in which they will spend the night time time.

The bodyguard, Rees-Jones, and Henri Paul on the the the front seat; Diana have become on the lower back beside Dodi Fayed who changed into hidden in the returned of Paul

- In the intervening time, Henri Paul went out of doors the hotel to speak with a number of the paparazzi that he knew. The type of photographers had stepped forward with the aid of the hour, eagerly looking for the couple to emerge from the hotel. Kes

Wingfield, the bodyguard, said that Dodi came up with a plan to idiot the photographers. There will be decoy motors to leave the front of the Ritz to lure the paparazzi away so he and Diana ought to interrupt out from the again and pass again efficaciously to his rental.

- It modified into already 12:20 am on August 31, 1997 at the same time as the Mercedes 220SL that contained the couple on the side of Henri Paul as the using pressure and Trevor Rees-Jones, a bodyguard, left the again company front of the motel. It changed into alleged that Henri Paul shouted to 3 paparazzi,

- "Don't problem following, you gained't capture us."

Some photographers have been capable of grasp a few images of Diana hiding her face in her arms as the auto sped away into the night time time.

- Henri Paul's cat-and-mouse chase with the paparazzi proved to be volatile, greater so due to the truth he was so inebriated that he emerge as 3 instances over the criminal restrict for ingesting and riding. It became moreover located out that he had taken an anti-depressant and every other drug to deal with his alcoholism. The aggregate have come to be a deadly one.

- Investigations after the twist of destiny may show that Paul end up 600 instances much more likely to have a lethal car crash with the quantity of alcohol in his bloodstream. Knowing that he changed into immoderate on drink, pills and adrenaline, he drove like a maniac. Dominic Lawson, editor of the Sunday Telegraph and a pal of Diana, said,

"Drunk or sober, no chauffeur would possibly adventure at over 100 miles constant with hour in a tunnel with a 30 miles in line with hour restrict, besides ordered to achieve this through his boss."

A photographer following the Mercedes claimed to have visible the auto beating a crimson mild on the Place de l. A. Concorde in the direction of the Place de l'Alma underpass at a excessive tempo. At approximately 12:24 am, at the price of 80 five to 95 miles an hour, the car entered the tunnel. The riding force misplaced manipulate and the auto collided head-on with the thirteenth pillar supporting the roof. The car skidded round and hit the wall of the tunnel backwards in advance than coming to a forestall.

The vehicle that carried Princess Diana and Dodi after the deadly coincidence

- The the the front of the auto changed into drastically broken. Dodi and Paul have been killed proper now while Rees-Jones suffered from a couple of important facial accidents however despite the fact that alive. He regained interest weeks later. Diana become sitting in the rear right passenger seat, no matter the reality that conscious. It become counseled that a photographer who became on the scene observed that Diana emerge as bleeding from the nose and ears. He had attempted to eliminate her from the car but she changed into trapped within the nicely among the back and front seats. The photographers who've been chasing them had been the number one ones on the scene and claimed to have heard a loud bang, questioning that Diana changed into the victim of an assassin's bomb.

A picture of the injured princess moments after the crash

- Federic Maillez, a health practitioner who occurred on the scene, finished emergency resource. Other medical assist arrived a piece later at the same time as a few paparazzi took their opportunities of snatching pics. Others cared quality about taking snap shots of the bloody scene and did no longer telephone for assist or consolation the loss of life princess. When the police arrived, that that that they had to call for reinforcements to deal with the paparazzi. Seven photographers were arrested and had been investigated for manslaughter and failure to assist the twist of fate sufferers.

- It become 1:00am while Diana have turn out to be pulled out from the wreckage, after which she went into cardiac arrest. Her coronary coronary heart beat all over again after outside cardiopulmonary resuscitation. She became taken into an ambulance at 1:18, which left the scene at 1:41. It arrived on the close by Pitie-Salpetriere Hospital at 2:06am.

- By then it emerge as too beyond because of preserve her. She suffered from large head and chest accidents. It modified into decided out that her coronary heart grow to be displaced from the left to the proper factor of the chest, tearing the pulmonary vein and the pericardium in the process. Diana had long gone thru inner and external coronary heart massage which lasted for two hours, but the attempt failed. Diana have grow to be declared useless at four:00am.

- Subsequent investigations into the twist of fate showed that most effective the bodyguard, Rees-Jones, wore a seatbelt. Some humans speculated that Diana's accidents can also were lots less excessive if she were wearing a seatbelt. The investigators additionally determined out how drunken Paul changed into.

Conspiracy Theories

In mild of the investigations following the accident, the French research concluded that Princess Diana died of her injuries from the car twist of fate. But first-class conspiracy theories had been constantly supplied, together with Mohamed Al-Fayed's concept that Diana turn out to be genuinely assassinated. He have become supported via the Daily Express. As a end result, a special inquest become ordered to analyze the conspiracy theorists. In 2004, the Operation Paget, headed with the resource of the then Commissioner Lord Stevens, investigated the conspiracy theories and suggested the findings years later.

Dodi's father, Mohamed Al Fayed, claiming that Diana changed into assassinated

- A 2007 inquest turn out to be moreover carried out under the supervision of Dame Elizabeth Butler-Sloss. But on April of the identical 365 days, Butler-Sloss stepped down, claiming she did now not have the enjoy to address the inquest with a jury. She was changed with the aid of Lord Justice Scott Baker.

- On March 31, 2008, Lord Baker stated that there has been no evidence to indicate that the Duke of Edinburgh ordered the dying of Diana or that the protection services had to do with it. He summed up the file on April 2, 2008, and on April 7, the jury determined that the grossly negligent driving of Henri Paul and the following motors had been what killed Diana.

The Royal Family's Reaction

The royal family modified into underneath the spotlight after Diana's death, but now not for extraordinary reasons. Their response to the news of Diana's demise brought on outcry from the public, specifically after studying that the circle of relatives modified into at Balmoral Castle. They did no longer go back to London right away or mourn publicly, and this changed into cautiously criticized at the time. Although they were adhering to their strict protocol and have been involved approximately William and Harry, the public misinterpreted it as lack of compassion.

- In fact, the Queen and Prince Charles were woken up through aides after studying of the statistics. Prince Charles listened to radio announcements the whole night time and informed his sons approximately the information within the morning. The own family stayed in seclusion at Balmoral days following Diana's death.

- But this reaction triggered further threats to the monarchy. Mary Francis, the Queen's private secretary, stated that the overall public anger closer to the royal own family's preliminary reaction to Diana's death may encourage the republican Member of Parliament to call for an prevent to the monarchy. She recalled that the courtiers were unwell-organized as they told her that Diana's family would in all likelihood need a private funeral. It come to be a mistake, and all hell broke free.

Newspapers' the front covers display how the general public felt

- Following the overall public's demand that the royal family should leave Balmoral, each other problem revolved round whether or not or not the Union Flag should be flown at

1/2 of mast on the Buckingham Palace. If the royal family did now not reply, the clamor may additionally have escalated to the factor of overthrowing the monarchy and calling for a republican motion.

- At first, at the same time as information of Diana's lack of existence became introduced, the u . S . Must not often take delivery of as proper with it. It seemed not possible. But the grieving country became its anger in competition to the royal own family. The circle of relatives had already been below fireside after Diana's revelations of her enjoy being a part of the circle of relatives, and her loss of life modified into another blow that threatened the monarchy. It hit them hard.

- A few days after the burial, the royal family spent the week in seclusion at Balmoral. The public emerge as short to word that in region of main the country in mourning, they retreated to their summer house. But the overall public's contamination with this reaction turn out to be now not new. In the past, in the path of failures and accidents which embody the Pan Am crash at Lockerbie, the royal own family was on holiday and did now not attend memorial services. They had been criticized for it, but the anger abated. This time, the outpouring of grief emerge as a large hazard.

- The u . S . A . Resented the own family as they were greater concerned to comply with the protocol in desire to the people's desires. Their selection to move on a holiday turn out to be a demonstration in their turning their backs on the country even as it wished them. The Sun posted a headline which pondered how the dominion felt: "Where is the Queen even as the usa of a desires her? She is 550 miles from London, the focal point of the u . S .'s grief." In response, it become introduced that the Queen should move returned to London to cope with the kingdom at the eve of the funeral.

The Public's Reaction and the Funeral

The BAe146 of the Queen's Flight bearing Diana's frame seemed to be the bloodless water poured into human beings's heads that made them actually take transport of that Diana have become definitely long lengthy past. As the aircraft approached the RAF Northolt at 7:00 of that nighttime, the enormity of Diana's loss sank in. Eight RAF pall bears carried Diana's coffin, draped with the Royal Standard and a wreath of white lilies. Her body turn out to be taken t a personal mortuary and then to St. James Palace.

A sea of plant life outdoor Kensington Palace

- The complete country and unique international locations as nicely mourned the days following the burial. The extensive kind of folks who flocked from round the arena grow to be a sworn declaration in their love and admire for the princess. The entire international witnessed an outpouring of grief as they introduced plant life, card, stuffed toys and all types of topics outside the gates of the Buckingham Palace and Kensington Palace.

- That the arena grieved for Diana modified into greater special. It became in no way seen earlier than. On the day of Diana's funeral, the area regarded to prevent revolving. The humans cried for their princess. They got here a long manner from their jobs, left what they have been doing and watched from their TV as Diana's coffin modified into delivered to Westminster Abbey.

On the day of her funeral, extra than 1,000,000 spectators included the 4-mile direction from Kensington Palace to Westminster Abbey. London grow to be preoccupied with the funeral procession and the rite to follow. Never modified into it so though in the america of the us. Shops have been close to. Planes were not allowed to fly over the city besides at an excessive top. And all sports occasions were cancelled to make way for the funeral. Not first-class the complete the united states but the international turned into in mourning for the "England's Rose."

11:08 am

The cortege left Kensington Palace. From then at the bell rang each minute till it arrived at Westminster Abbey. The princess' coffin lay on a gun carriage. The blue-red-gold royal desired became wrapped over the coffin. During the procession, the people need to cry and scream "Diana, Diana..." over and over yet again. Twelve participants of the Welsh Guard from the Princess of Wales' regiment, adorned in purple jackets and black bearskin hats, stood on each factor of the coffin.

12:09 pm

Queen Elizabeth and her sons, Prince Edward and Prince Andrew, alongside facet

Princess Margaret, Fergie and her daughters and some ladies-in-prepared stood outside Buckingham Palace to count on the funeral procession.

12:18 pm

The cortege reached the royal palace. The Queen silently bowed as quickly as in advance than her vain former daughter-in-regulation. The cortege persevered on its manner on the equal time because the Queen again to the palace.

12:23 pm

The cortege reached St. James' Palace, Charles' house. Here Prince Charles, Prince William, Prince Harry, Charles Spencer and Prince Philip, all sporting black suits with black ties, waited and walked behind the cortege, and in the back of them marched the 5 hundred individuals of charities that Princess Diana supported.-

- The facets of the streets were crowded with spectators, a number of whom added cardboard placards showing "Diana, we love you" and "Good-bye Diana."Flags of all international locations lined the streets.

12:44pm

Queen Elizabeth left Buckingham Palace. The Union Jack flag is probably seen flown at half of-mast, some thing that England have been looking forward to. Invited traffic also saved arriving at the coronation church.

1:00pm

More than 1000 mourners filled Westminster Abbey. Ten minutes in advance, the Queen arrived. The countrywide anthem turned into sung, after which all eyes were regular at the church portal. Eight Welsh Guards carried the coffin interior. They set it down in advance than the altar. Four big candles stood on 4 corners. Queen Elizabeth, Prince Philip, Prince Charles and his sons laid down white bouquets of vegetation. The funeral carrier began out.

- Diana's two sisters, Lady Sarah and Lady Jane, gave short speeches. Prime Minister Tony Blair observe an excerpt from the primary letter to the Corinthians. Among the excessive factors of the funeral become while Elton John, one in each of Diana's near pals, sang "Candle inside the Wind," starting with a "Goodbye England's Rose" in memory of Diana. While he sang, Prince William and Prince Harry cried, and the agency out of doors the church cried as nicely. For masses of the track, the cameras did now not recognition on the grieving family people.

- Next modified into Charles Spencer's speech, which blamed the paparazzi for the tragic twist of destiny and at a loss for words the royal circle of relatives's remedy of the princess. Etiquette grow to be neglected because of the fact the congregation broke into applause, as did the humans outside the Abbey. Archbishop George Carey additionally gave a speech.

2:00pm

The provider ended. The 8 guards carried the coffin out of doors and positioned it in a black hearse which might in all likelihood take the coffin to the Althorp belongings. The limousine drove slowly through the streets of London, and the people threw flowers at the roof, at the bumper and at the bonnet.

5:30pm

Diana reached her home. The wrought-iron gate of Althorp closed at the back of her for the final time.

6:00pm

Diana have become buried with Prince Charles, Prince William, Prince Harry, Diana's siblings, her mother, a priest and Diana's best buddy in attendance. Inside the coffin lay Diana in a black get dressed, and in her fingers she held a rosary that Mother Theresa had given her as a present.

The hearse arrives at Althorp, in which Diana became buried

- More than seven hundred million watched her wedding ceremony on July 21, 1989, and a couple of.Five billion humans round the arena watched her funeral. The global emerge as in mourning. The following days witnessed human beings going to Buckingham Palace and Kensington to put flora for Diana. There had been people of every age and nationalities, the disabled, the lonely, the curious, the travelers and refugees. Diana have become the most effective person who changed into capable to connect with the people who've been rejected by using the society. In handiest every week, the courtyards became a sea of plants with greater than one million laid there.

Chapter 13: Commemorating Princess Di

Years after Diana's lack of life, she have become notwithstanding the reality that remembered and revered with the aid of way of people round the world. She modified into now not only for the Great Britain. Although she lived an extravagant lifestyles as Princess of Wales, she were given on extra with those who lived on the fringes of the society – the AIDS patients, the lepers, and the tons an awful lot much less lucky human beings.

Diana, Princess of Wales' memory lives on

- Diana left the area, but not with out legacies. Her being ranked 1/3 in the 2002 100 Greatest Britons ballot was more than a evidence of her lasting memory. The worldwide did no longer forget about her or all of the subjects she did. She can also have no longer positioned proper love, but the humans cherished her.

Diana's existence may be summed up thru the Prime Minister's speech:

"She touched the lives of such lots of others in Britain and within the course of the sector with joy and with consolation. How difficult subjects were for her every now and then, I', sure we will fine guess at. But human beings everywhere, now not sincerely proper right here in Britain, saved religion with Princess Diana. They preferred her, they cherished her, they appeared her as one of the people. She have grow to be the People's Princess and that is how she can live, how she may be able to stay in all our hearts and recollections forever."

www.ingramcontent.com/pod-product-compliance
Lightning Source LLC
Chambersburg PA
CBHW071446080526
44587CB00014B/2006